D0292302

Jules Archer
History for Young Readers

FRONTLINE GENERAL:
DOUGLAS MacARTHUR

AMERICA'S MOST
CONTROVERSIAL HERO

JULES ARCHER

Foreword by Iain C. Martin

Sky Pony Press
NEW YORK

Historical texts often reflect the time period in which they were written, and new information is constantly being discovered. This book was originally published in 1964, and much has changed since then. While every effort has been made to bring this book up to date, it is important to consult multiple sources when doing research.

Sky Pony Press books may be purchased in bulk at special discounts for sales promotion, corporate gifts, fund-raising, or educational purposes. Special editions can also be created to specifications. For details, contact the Special Sales Department, Sky Pony Press, 307 West 36th Street, 11th Floor, New York, NY 10018 or info@skyhorsepublishing.com.

Sky Pony® is a registered trademark of Skyhorse Publishing, Inc.®, a Delaware corporation.

Visit our website at www.skyponypress.com.

10 9 8 7 6 5 4 3 2 1

Library of Congress Cataloging-in-Publication Data is available on file.

Series design by Brian Peterson
Cover photo credit Associated Press

Print ISBN: 978-1-63450-168-2
Ebook ISBN: 978-1-5107-0698-9

Printed in the United States of America

To the beloved members of my private army—Eleanor, Mike, Dane, Kerry, and Mom—who had a personal stake in the MacArthur victories at Milne Bay and Markham Valley.

Grateful acknowledgment is made to Mr. Paul B. Basco, administrative aide to General MacArthur, for supplying firsthand information and comment from the General to clarify some points raised by the author.

The author is indebted to Pyramid Publications for permission to adapt in different form the author's account of MacArthur's adventure in Mexico, and also the Buna affair, both of which originally appeared in *Man's Magazine*.

For the chapters dealing with World War II in Australia, New Guinea, and the Philippines, the author has also drawn upon his personal experiences during four years in the Pacific.

A special debt of gratitude is owed to the author's wife Eleanor, to Miss Edith Margolis, and to Dr. Randolph G. Goodman of Brooklyn College, for their invaluable support and help en route.

Jules Archer
Pine Plains,
New York

CONTENTS

FOREWORD

Duty, Honor, Country

Few leaders in American history have been more revered, mistrusted, and feared than General Douglas MacArthur. He was hailed by many as an iconic leader, a genius for war who accomplished seemingly impossible tasks with few resources. Yet he was distrusted by those who saw his vanity and the carefully crafted public image as the trappings of a charlatan. President Franklin Roosevelt once famously quipped that Douglas MacArthur was the second most dangerous man in America after Huey Long (a firebrand populist political rival of FDR). MacArthur's thinly veiled political ambitions inspired trepidation in some, and strong support from others. Many Americans anticipated he might capitalize on his fame to make the final leap from military command to the White House.

Douglas was born into an Army life at the Arsenal Barracks in Little Rock, Arkansas on January 26, 1880. His father, Arthur MacArthur Jr. was an Army captain from Massachusetts who, as a young man, won the Medal of Honor during the Civil War at Missionary Ridge. Arthur eventually became the Military Governor of the Philippines, and later the commander of the Department of the Pacific. His mother, Mary Pinkney Hardy MacArthur, was an educated southern belle from Norfolk, Virginia. Together they instilled in the young MacArthur a love of country, a sense of duty, and a belief that he was destined for greatness like his father. His service would begin at the twilight of the western frontier before the age of flight and end fifty-two years later just before the first intercontinental nuclear missiles would change warfare forever.

Douglas wasted no time in blazing a path to command. Gifted with a genius intellect, a commanding personality, a famous name, and a strong physique, MacArthur's future seemed assured. As a cadet at West Point he achieved the highest honors, making First Captain at the top of his class of 1903. During the First World War he won glory as a front line officer with the 42nd "Rainbow" Division in France. Promoted to Brigadier General at the age of thirty-nine, he became the youngest superintendent of the West Point Military Academy since its founding.

At West Point MacArthur instituted much needed reforms to improve the cadet's education beyond military science. Recognizing that future generals would also need to undertake civil and diplomatic missions, the curriculum was expanded. Douglas also emphasized the importance of sports as a cornerstone of building teamwork and character. "Every cadet an athlete" became a consequential goal. On MacArthur's order this maxim was carved into the stone portals of the academy gymnasium, "On the fields of friendly strife are sown the seeds that on other days, on other fields will bear the fruits of victory."

As America's youngest Major General at the age of fifty he became the Army's Chief of Staff and oversaw a reorganization of the Army and the implementation of President Roosevelt's Civilian Conservation Corps. When Congress approved the formation of the CCC in March 1933, Roosevelt hoped to have 250,000 men enrolled in work camps across the country by July. Only with the Army's help was such a goal possible and the task was given to MacArthur. By July the general had three hundred thousand men enrolled, thus making the CCC one of Roosevelt's key New Deal success stories.

At the age of fifty-five MacArthur agreed to oversee the creation of the Philippine Army for President Manuel Quezon. To this end, he was allowed to assume the rank of Field Marshall of the Philippine Army. MacArthur also retained his status as a Major General in the United States Army and the official US advisor for the island nation.

His career by then would have been deemed accomplished by any measure yet his greatest challenges still lay ahead. When Japanese bombers attacked the Philippines on December 8, 1941 most American aircraft were caught on the ground and destroyed. Following the Japanese invasion of Luzon, MacArthur fought a delaying action while his forces retreated onto the Bataan peninsula where they dug in. MacArthur and his forces awaited Allied reinforcements for months, but with no relief forthcoming, President Roosevelt instead ordered MacArthur to evacuate to Australia where he would lead an eventual counterattack.

In an audacious eleven-day escape that began on March 12, 1942 from Corregidor Island, MacArthur and his family evaded capture thanks to daring PT boats and aircraft. Stunned on his arrival in Australia that no Allied army awaited him, MacArthur vowed to reporters on his intent to avenge the loss of the Philippines, "I came through and I shall return." Here was a glimpse of the real MacArthur, who on his own initiative, proclaimed the military goals of the United States without consulting Washington. When officially asked to amend his statement to "we shall return" MacArthur ignored the request. In the United States MacArthur was proclaimed a hero and was awarded his long-sought-after Medal of Honor to shield him from any disgrace.

The stage was now set for a military campaign to turn the tide of Japanese conquest and advance the Allies toward Japan. MacArthur was appointed Supreme Commander of Allied Forces in the Southwest Pacific Area on 18 April, 1942. Using all his abilities as a statesman and a soldier, and learning hard lessons along the way, McArthur led an island-hopping strategy from the jungles of New Guinea, up through the Solomon Islands all the way back to the beaches of Leyte in the Philippines. When MacArthur triumphantly waded ashore on October 20, 1944 he addressed the Philippine people by radio from the beach, "People of the Philippines: I have returned. . . ."

On September 2, 1945 MacArthur officiated the Japanese surrender aboard the USS *Missouri* in Tokyo Bay. In his speech, perhaps his finest moment, MacArthur brought grace to a day of shame for the Japanese. "It is my earnest hope, and indeed the hope of all mankind, that from this solemn occasion a better world shall emerge out of the blood and carnage of the past—a world dedicated to the dignity of man and the fulfillment of his most cherished wish for freedom, tolerance, and justice."

It was with this same measured tolerance that MacArthur ruled Japan for the next eight years as the Supreme Commander of Allied Forces. While exonerating the Emperor and his family from prosecution, MacArthur swept away the roots of Japanese militarism starting with the Tokyo War Crimes Tribunal. His reforms affected all levels of society as he gave women the right to vote, introduced land reform, broke up industrial monopolies, and allowed labor unions. MacArthur rewrote the Japanese constitution, outlawing the use of military force as national policy. The Japanese nicknamed him "Gaijin Shogun" (The Foreign Generalissimo).

In the final chapter of his military career MacArthur was unanimously recommended by the Joint Chiefs of Staff to lead a defense of the Korean peninsula, which had come under attack by communist forces on June 25, 1950. After his United Nations forces were forced to retreat southward into a perimeter around Pusan, MacArthur executed a risky amphibious landing on the western shore at Inchon, routing the enemy. As UN units advanced northwards past the 38th parallel there was a growing concern that China would enter the war. In late November the Chinese launched a surprise attack with an army of three hundred thousand men that recaptured Seoul and sent UN forces reeling southward.

The Korean War threatened to become a wider conflict, one that might involve nuclear weapons and could weaken America's position in western Europe. MacArthur's desire for total victory clashed with President Truman's policy of limited action and the containment of Communist states. When MacArthur made public statements opposing limited war and urging the removal of restrictions on his operations against the Chinese, he directly challenged Truman. The President was forced to relieve MacArthur of his command on April 10, 1951. The general returned to the United States a hero while Truman's approval ratings fell to twenty-two percent, the lowest of any American president. Truman chose not to seek re-election in 1952.

MacArthur ended his fifty-two years of service with the largest ticker tape parade through Manhattan in American history, drawing seven million spectators on April 20, 1951. The previous day he addressed a joint session of Congress: "I am closing my fifty-two years of military service. When I joined the Army, even before the turn of the century, it was the fulfillment of all of my boyish hopes and dreams. The world has turned over many times since I took the oath at West Point, and the hopes and dreams have all since vanished, but I still remember the refrain of one of the most popular barracks ballads of that day which proclaimed most proudly that old soldiers never die; they just fade away. And like the old soldier of that ballad, I now close my military career and just fade away, an old soldier who tried to do his duty as God gave him the light to see that duty."

Years later, as his health was failing, he gave an epic speech at West Point on May 12, 1962 that would inspire generations of future leaders. "The shadows are lengthening for me. The twilight is here. My days of old have vanished, tone and tint. They have gone glimmering through the dreams of things that were. Their memory is one of wondrous beauty, watered by tears, and coaxed and caressed by the smiles of yesterday. I listen vainly, but with thirsty ears, for the witching melody of faint bugles blowing reveille, of far drums beating the long roll. In my dreams I hear again the crash of guns, the rattle of musketry, the strange, mournful mutter of the battlefield. But in the evening of my memory, always I come back to West Point. Always there echoes and re-echoes: Duty, Honor, Country."

In the final days before his passing on April 5, 1964, MacArthur advised President Lyndon B. Johnson as he had advised President John F. Kennedy before him, to avoid a US military build-up in Vietnam. He warned against committing ground forces to support South Vietnam or anywhere else on mainland Asia. The ailing general advised that domestic issues should take a higher priority than the Vietnam crisis.

The half century since MacArthur's passing has allowed historians time to sift through the complex record of his legacy and shed light on the man behind his carefully crafted legend. What we discover is a complex man with deeply held convictions that he had a destiny to fulfill that no enemy bullet could deny him. Brimming with supreme confidence born of innate talents and a dominating personality, MacArthur was what one biographer termed the "American Caesar." Perhaps the best summation of the truth about Douglas MacArthur came from his Australian ground commander, General Thomas Blamey, who said, "the best and the worst things you hear about him are both true."

MacArthur's greatest achievements were accomplished by a mastery of logistics and an ability to adapt rapidly changing technologies into his strategy, cast over an expanse of the globe breathtaking in scope. His ability to achieve victories with marginal forces in the most difficult terrain in the far reaches of the southwest Pacific earned him a reputation as one of the greatest Allied generals of World War II. His greatest failures, the result of a dominating ego fed by paranoia, led to his shameless manipulation of the truth with the press and in official dispatches, and to his undermining of civilian authority of the military. MacArthur's belief that only his course of action was correct at all times forced him to trust only those whose loyalty was exclusively to him.

It is not without irony that MacArthur's career would end in a conflict with President Truman defying the very government he had sworn to defend. History has come to view MacArthur as a flawed genius, a cautionary example of vast individual power unchecked by superiors and the necessity of civilian leadership over military leadership. Yet it cannot be denied that MacArthur was a military genius, with a rare collection of abilities as a statesman and a soldier, and a champion of the American nation that he so loved. He remains one of the most accomplished and greatest Americans of the twentieth century.

—Iain C. Martin 2017

I

Seed-Bed of Heroes

Sawing the reins of his spotted Navajo pony, six-year-old Doug MacArthur came to an abrupt halt that cascaded hot white sand against the vibrantly blue New Mexico sky. His brother Arthur, nine, stood up in the stirrups and pointed excitedly.

"There! See? A camel—just like I said!"

The smaller boy stared at the strange phenomenon, suppressing his astonishment. He had grown conditioned to surprises in the Apache country on the New Mexico–Texas frontier. But *camels?*

"Look out!" Arthur shouted. "He's coming at us!"

Wheeling his pony, he started trotting back across the La Jornada del Muerto, the desert the Spaniards called the Journey of Death, toward the low adobe buildings of tiny, isolated Fort Seldon. But Doug remained rooted, impressed at how much bigger and more alarming real camels were than picture camels. Although his heart was pounding, his face showed no trace of apprehension. The massive beast halted uncertainly a few feet away.

Boy and camel stared at each other. Then the beast threw its head back and snorted, baring enormous teeth. Doug felt the blood drain from his cheeks. Raising himself in the saddle, he shook his small fist over his head defiantly, and tried to look as threatening as he could.

"Yahhhh!" he trilled savagely.

The startled dromedary staggered away to one side and turned its rump to Doug, lumbering off back across the desert toward the San Andres Range west of the Mescalero Apache reservation.

"Hey, Doug! Come on—let's tell Sergeant Baker!"

Racing their ponies, the two boys were back at Fort Seldon in less than twenty minutes. A sweat-soaked soldier listened to their breathless story as he hitched mules to a water wagon.

"A camel, eh?" Sergeant Baker sprang up on the buckboard and turned the mules toward a windswept bend of the Rio Grande. He regarded the brothers gravely. "I wouldn't exactly tell your daddy about it, if I was you boys."

Doug looked puzzled. "Why not?"

"Well, *I* believe you, a-course. But y'see, *he* thinks ain't nothin' in that desert 'ceptin' blue elephants!"

The boys stared after the water wagon as it drove off.

"Doug, you think Father won't believe us either?"

"He'll believe us!" Doug said indignantly. "He knows we wouldn't lie to him about an important thing like *that!*"

They found their father in his office, trying on a new hooded ulster coat for Army officers that had come with a mounted detachment from Fort Stanton.

"Like it, boys?" he smiled, turning around for them.

"It makes you look so *big!*" Doug said in surprise. Captain Arthur MacArthur's small stature had been a source of amusement to the Union forces he had joined at Louisville nineteen years earlier. The 24th Wisconsin Infantry had dubbed the seventeen-year-old lieutenant "the Little Adjutant," but their derision had swiftly changed to profound admiration for "the Brave Little Devil." He had fought with such ferocity and bravery at Missionary Ridge that Generals Sheridan and Grant had both praised him, and he had been awarded the Congressional Medal of Honor.

"Big, eh?" Captain MacArthur laughed. "Well, you always want to look big to your men—and to the enemy, too. Shows them both you're not afraid to be a target!"

He listened thoughtfully as they told him about the camel.

"And we're not making it up, Father!" Doug said fervently.

"I know you're not, son, because there *are* camels in these parts. When Jefferson Davis was Secretary of War about thirty years ago, he imported a herd of them from Egypt to supply the forts out here in desert country. He thought they might work out better than pack animals. But they made a lot of enemies because they had nasty tempers and bit everybody, so the Army finally turned them loose in the desert."

"What happened to them?" Arthur asked.

"Nobody knows. I guess you boys ran across a survivor."

"I chased it away, Father!" Doug said fiercely. "It was big as a mountain, but I wasn't scared a bit!"

"Naturally," his father said. "You're a MacArthur."

The earliest sound Douglas MacArthur remembered hearing was a bugle call. He was born at one military post, raised at another, and devoured books about military heroes. His playmates were soldiers' sons who fought Cavalry-Indian battles with him on barracks drillfields. Every evening when the flag came down he stood retreat with the company, stiffly at attention, and drilled alongside them in the army square. Stirred by the daily thunder of guns, drums and bugles, it never occurred to him to be anything but a soldier when he grew up.

He spent his early boyhood surrounded by rugged men whose daily business was heroism. Wild Bill Hickok and Buffalo Bill were both friends of his father. Young Doug listened enthralled to the tales of Indian scouts, cavalrymen and frontiersmen who galloped into the post fresh from battles, raids, and skirmishes. When he was only four he had a wildly exciting adventure of his own. Geronimo's Apaches had suddenly swooped down upon Fort Seldon from the Mescalero reservation beyond the San Andres Range. Doug had been playing with lead soldiers in the shadowed sand near the garrison stable when flaming arrows began raining into the fort. One of them plunked into the sand inches away from his outthrust leg. Too shocked to cry out, Doug suddenly felt himself scooped up by an Army sergeant who raced him toward safety. His mother came flying out of her house, snatched him from the soldier, then dashed toward the door with her back to the flaming arrows.

The incident gave him his first sense of identity with his father. Captain Arthur MacArthur, riding at the head of Company K, 13th Infantry, had narrowly escaped death during four different Indian battles in Wyoming Territory.

"Never be afraid," he told his sons. "Or if you are, don't show it. Just keep your mind on your duty at all times, and remember that we MacArthurs have charmed lives in battle!"

"I'm beginning to believe it myself," Doug's mother assured them. "Your father comes from a long line of famous Scottish warriors. There are records to prove they fought in the Crusades and under Robert Bruce for Scotland's freedom. And a famous Scot proverb says, 'Nothing has stood longer than MacArthur, the hills, and the devil.' Your father seems to be just as indestructible as his ancestors. Here, let me show you something."

She produced an old packet of letters pierced by a charred bullet hole. Doug and Arthur examined them curiously.

"During the Civil War," she explained, "your father led the 24th Wisconsin Regiment in a bayonet charge up Kenesaw Mountain. He was badly wounded in the leg, bleeding a lot, but he refused to stop fighting. Then a Rebel bullet struck him right over the heart. But it didn't kill him because it couldn't tear through that pack of letters he kept in his left breast pocket!"

Doug MacArthur never forgot that proof of the indestructibility of the MacArthurs on the battlefield. All through his military career his cool daring and incredible fearlessness under fire had roots in his profound conviction that he also could not be killed in action.

If he had his father's example to inspire him, he also had the climate of courage provided by his mother. Mary Pinkney Hardy had been a pretty Southern belle of twenty-three when she met Captain Arthur MacArthur in 1875 at a Mardi Gras in New Orleans, near Jackson Post where he had been stationed after seven rugged years of fighting in the Indian badlands.

The handsome young couple fell in love and announced their intention to marry. Mary Hardy's four brothers, all Confederate veterans, roared their protest. They warned her that if she tried to bring a Yankee soldier into the family, they would refuse to attend her wedding. Although she loved her brothers she defied them, and they boycotted the ceremony.

Holding her chin high, Mary MacArthur followed her husband west from one bleak frontier post to another. She found little female companionship. The rigors of Army post life had small appeal for most women. But despite an aristocratic upbringing on a North Carolina plantation, Mary MacArthur adjusted to every hardship without a tear or complaint.

Her first son, Arthur MacArthur III, was born in 1876. A second son died of the measles. Douglas MacArthur was born at the military post in Little Rock, Arkansas, on January 26, 1880. Like many youngest sons, Doug quickly became his mother's favorite, and he, in turn, was completely devoted to her. In her own way, Mary MacArthur was to affect the course of world history through her great influence over her son.

"You," she is alleged to have told Doug, "are going to be the greatest MacArthur of them all!" It was flattering and inspiring, but it implied also being bound by a frightening obligation.

Doug's first lesson in Spartan fortitude also came from his mother. Shortly after the Apache attack on Fort Seldon he was awakened in the middle of the night by the growing, ominous throb of Indian drums from across the moonlit Jornada Del Muerto. The memory of flaming arrows was still terrifyingly vivid, and five-year-old Doug began to sob. When his mother came to his bed it was not to console him, but to admonish him gently for his "unmanly" behavior.

"I've seen Father cry," Doug protested, "when the bugle is playing and they lower the flag at night."

"That's different, dear," she explained. "A man is allowed to cry out of patriotic feeling, but out of fear—*never!*"

For as long as he could remember, Doug had always taken it for granted that he and Arthur were headed for West Point. They never suffered from the lack of formal schools to attend because their parents were superb teachers. At each new military post, the boys' quarters were converted into a private schoolroom. Mother taught them basic subjects, along with the social polish expected of military gentlemen. Doug also acquired from her a lifelong taste for elegance in dress.

Whenever Father returned from Indian skirmishes, he also took a hand in his sons' education. Outdoors he trained them as skilled horsemen, expert shots, and adroit plainsmen. Indoors he read aloud to them from the lives of great military heroes— Captain MacArthur's own idols. Eyes shining as he lay on the floor with his chin propped on his fists, Doug determined that one day *his* life too would be in such books.

"I can't wait any more to get to West Point," he told his brother enthusiastically. "Can you?"

"I'm not going to West Point, Doug," Arthur said. "I've decided to make a career in the Navy instead."

Doug was stunned and incredulous. He stared at Arthur as though his brother had announced his intention to reject American citizenship. "But—why?" he gasped.

Arthur shrugged and stared restlessly across the monotonous desert that stretched away emptily into the purple sky. "I guess I'm sick of being land-bound. I want to go to sea."

Captain MacArthur was stung by Arthur's decision at first, taking it almost as a personal rejection of his own way of life. But he was an intelligent man and recognized that Arthur might be suffering in the shadow of his military achievements during the Civil War and in the West, needing to strike out on a path for himself where he could not be compared with his father.

With good grace Captain MacArthur helped his older son obtain an appointment to Annapolis. A short while later, upon their father's promotion to major, the MacArthurs were transferred to Fort Houston. Deciding that it was time for thirteen-year-old Doug to get some formal schooling, Mrs. MacArthur entered him in day sessions of the West Texas Military Academy.

She wanted him back in the fort every evening so that he might continue to be exposed to the influence of his father. Major MacArthur had undertaken intensive studies in political economy and history. Soon much of this knowledge began rubbing off on Doug's inquiring mind.

"Doug," his father told him, "the higher you rise in the military, the more opportunity you will have to make mistakes. Never be ashamed to take advice from strategists who know more than you do. I've had two advisers I always listen to. Would you like them as your personal advisers, too?"

"Sure!" Doug said eagerly. "Do I know them?"

"Possibly. Man named Washington, and one called Lincoln."

Doug grinned. "If they were good enough for you, Father, they're certainly good enough for me!" And they were. He pored over every book about them he could get his hands on. Years later, when he baffled his staff by referring to "my advisers," they were even more perplexed to find out who these were.

Doug's four-year average at West Texas was an extraordinary 97.33 percent, earning him the Academy's gold medal for "extraordinary excellence in scholarship and deportment." His intense drive to excel spilled over into sports as well, and he played shortstop as well as managing the baseball team to four successive years as league champions. "He was a born leader," one fellow student recalled later. "Every other boy took orders from him. And yet he was never dictatorial. He simply told us what we were going to do—and we did it."

Doug also persisted in trying out for the football squad, although he was told he was too light, until the coach finally gave in and placed him at quarterback. "The scrimmages were hard on him," said Garahl Walker, another classmate. "You could see his lips turn blue, but he would get up and fight it again!"

Doug graduated as valedictorian of the class of 1897. A year later his father was promoted to the rank of general and ordered to the Philippines to attack the Spanish garrisons at Manila. Mary MacArthur took Doug to Milwaukee, where her husband's relatives had been living since 1849. Here he sat for the competitive examination for an appointment to West Point, scoring an amazing 99 percent against 77.9 percent for his closest competitor. Doug was understandably jubilant, and began packing to leave for the Academy.

Then his hopes were dealt a cruel blow. The Academy informed him regretfully that he could not be accepted because the physical examination revealed a slight spinal ailment.

Doug was furious. "Of all the darn fool red tape!" he spluttered to his mother. "All right, they can go to blazes—the devil with the Army! I'll go to Annapolis, like Arthur!"

His mother calmed him down. "Don't cut off your nose to spite your face, Douglas. The sensible thing to do is to cure that spinal ailment. We're going to see Dr. Franz Pfister, one of the best doctors in Milwaukee!"

Dr. Pfister told them treatment would take a full year, and he couldn't guarantee results unless Doug promised to obey orders to the letter. The boy clenched his teeth and agreed. Dr. Pfister found him as good as his word. Not only that, but Doug also showed a vivid interest in anatomy, biology, physiology, and everything that concerned health and medical science. Dr. Pfister shook his head.

"Ach, Douglas, what a waste! West Point—*phui!* You should be going to Harvard Medical School! You would make a great physician and surgeon!"

In 1899, cured of his spinal trouble and finally accepted by West Point, Doug thrilled as the golden doors to military glory swung open to him. He marched through them jubilantly, rejoicing in his mother's great pride, excited that his lifelong dream was coming true. He knew how happy the news would make his father, when the cable his mother had sent reached Manila.

MacArthur Senior was celebrating a triumph of his own, having scored a stunning victory over an insurgent army led by General Aguinaldo. He now wore three stars, and President McKinley had appointed him first American military governor of the Philippines. Doug was understandably proud. He didn't realize that his father's growing fame made him a marked man.

Inside the Academy the whole student body awaited the arrival of the son of Lieutenant General Arthur MacArthur, hero of Manila. In the months to come, Doug often had occasion to regret that his name wasn't John Smith, and that his father didn't own the shabby little fruit store around the corner.

2

MacArthur Captures
West Point

The melancholy serenade to sunset floated out across the Hudson from the tents of the Academy's summer camp. At the last lingering note Doug took a deep breath, pushed aside the flap of a tent at the edge of Company A, and entered.

"Cadet Douglas MacArthur reporting as ordered."

The six upperclassmen in the tent exchanged glances. Cadet Barry, a hard-mouthed bantam who walked tall, circled Doug's erect figure with an imperceptible smile that held no warmth. "Well, gentlemen! This *is* an occasion! I'm sure I don't have to tell you that our distinguished visitor is the son of Lieutenant General Arthur MacArthur, whose brave exploits in Luzon thrill us every day in the headlines."

Their faces straight, the other five yearlings bowed deeply to the newcomer. Doug colored faintly, already steeled to this kind of irony. Often at dinner, just as he prepared to eat his first forkful, he was ordered to stand and describe his father's feats of derring-do in the Civil War and the Philippines.

Barry clasped his hands behind him in mock solemnity and continued to circle Doug like a biology professor lecturing with an anatomical model. "And I think you are aware, gentlemen, that Mister MacArthur has the unique distinction of being the first cadet whose mother is going through the Academy with him."

The third classmen snickered, and Doug s jaw muscles tensed at this reference to his mother having taken up residence at the old West Point Hotel to be near her son. He could endure the hazing in scalding steam baths, standing at rigid attention for an hour, or doing endless knee-bends while naked in a circle of broken glass, but mockery of his mother was unbearable. It was hard to retain self-control.

Noting the icy anger which chilled Doug's wide-set brown eyes, Barry smiled thinly in satisfaction. "But Mister MacArthur is not here, gentlemen, because he is a snob on his father's side and a mama's boy on his mother's. No, indeed! Nor are we reproaching him for showing off with the highest score ever made on entrance exams in the history of the Academy."

The five other cadets shook their heads gravely.

"Mister MacArthur," Barry sighed, "you grieve us deeply because of your failure to brace properly."

Doug clenched his teeth, fully aware that his was the most erect figure at the Academy. A lifetime of military preparation had made it impossible for him to walk or stand in a slouch.

"You may have your choice of a calling-out fight with members of the yearling class boxing squad, or of accepting discipline. Which do you prefer, Mister?"

Doug hesitated. Nothing at that moment would have given him more satisfaction than beating Barry's sneering face to a pulp. But Point tradition did not allow him to choose his opponent, and the likelihood was that Barry was not one of the third-classmen on the boxing squad. Furthermore, even if a plebe did manage to beat his opponent, he was then required to keep fighting other yearlings until he was finally knocked out himself. Thinking of how shocked his mother would be at his appearance after a brutal beating like this, and the painful explanation he would have to make to her, he made his decision.

"Discipline," he said crisply.

"Discipline, *Mister Barry!*" his tormentor barked.

Doug clenched his fists. "Discipline, Mister Barry."

"All right, Mister. Start eagling—and keep going!"

Taking a deep breath, MacArthur began doing knee-bends in a rigid military posture, with the precision and grace of a born athlete. The six yearlings watched in silent amazement as he lowered and rose fifty times, then seventy, then a hundred, in perfect rhythm with the ticking of a clock on Barry's cot table. When sweat began blinding him, Doug shut his eyes and kept going in the cadence, controlling his breathing to keep from panting. One hundred fifty . . . two hundred . . . how long, oh Lord?

"For God's sake, Barry!" one shocked cadet protested. "Shut up. Keep going, Mister!"

His uniform wringing wet, every muscle protesting in agony, Doug forced himself on grimly. With a supreme effort he went on to the count of two hundred fifty.

Then with a stifled moan he collapsed, pitching forward on the damp earth floor which spread its merciful coolness to the steaming perspiration that drenched him from head to foot.

One yearling whistled. "Wow, that's a record!"

Looking discountenanced, Barry threw a pail of water over the sprawling figure. Doug sat up painfully, shook his head and rose to his feet which were so weak they hardly held him.

"You stopped before I told you to, Mister!" Barry rasped. "That calls for hanging from a stretcher. Start hanging!"

Shaking his head again to clear his vision, Doug inhaled deeply and sprang up, gripping the tent pole as high as he could reach, and hung there with grim determination. His body seemed like a giant weight pulling at his wrists. Perspiration making his hands slippery, he fought to keep his feet from touching the ground. Each moment seemed an eternity, and he tried not to hate the upper-classmen who were doing this to him. Enduring the terrible pain in his arms and shoulders as long as he could, he finally fell in a heap.

"For Pete's sake, Barry, that's enough!" a yearling protested uneasily. "What are you trying to do—kill him"?"

Barry's eyes glittered with smoldering rage as he lifted Doug's sweaty chin with the toe of his boot. "Had enough, Mister? Want to beg us to let you off?"

MacArthur's head went back limply against the pole, his eyes glazed but defiant, lips firmly sealed. The tent was beginning to swirl around him now.

Infuriated by his inability to break the spirit of his stubborn victim, Barry yelled, "All *right,* Mister! Since you insist on being so all-fired tough, start dipping!"

Doug wearily fought off the waves of unconsciousness lapping at him, and forced himself into a series of push-ups. His arms began to quiver violently, protesting their utter fatigue. In the effort to hold out, he bit his lip until blood poured down his chin. Then with a groan his face fell to the earth.

"Barry, he looks bad—"

"Don't let the agony act fool you, gentlemen. If he's had enough, all he has to do is say so! What about it, Mister MacArthur? Still playing hero? All right, then, Mister, let's have some more eagling. And this time *pep it up!*"

The torture lasted for another hour. Incensed at Doug's stubborn refusal to beg for mercy, Barry became more and more frenzied in his cruelty until at last the other yearlings felt compelled to insist that he let MacArthur go. The victim of their hazing staggered out of the tent into the gathering dusk, barely able to stay on his feet.

When he reached his own tent and reeled inside, his tentmate, Fred Cunningham, caught him as he fell. Shocked at Doug's appearance, Cunningham lowered him to the earth gently. MacArthur's body began to convulse, his legs writhing and twisting so violently that he was afraid the thumping would bring company officers to investigate. He begged Cunningham to hold his feet still, and when this didn't work asked him to put a blanket under them to muffle the sounds.

Then severe cramps stabbed at Doug's abdomen, and he bit the back of his hand. "If I cry out," he urged Cunningham, "stuff the blanket in my mouth."

Later that evening his six tormentors, worried about having gone too far, stole into MacArthur's tent to check on his condition. Barry, now contrite, sent a plebe to the tank for a bucket of water and washed Doug's dirt-streaked face himself.

"Don't take this for any kind of an apology," he said curtly, "because we don't have to apologize for hazing plebes. I just want to say you've got guts. You're no Mama's boy!"

In the morning, a mass of aches from head to toe, Doug could hardly get off his cot. Fred Cunningham urged him to go on sick report but MacArthur refused, turning out for drill and the day's duties just as though nothing had happened.

When the word spread through the whole corps, Doug was regarded with new respect, no longer a target because of his too-celebrated father. But Fred Cunningham was so disgusted by the senseless cruelty of the hazing system that had victimized MacArthur, he resigned from the Academy six weeks later.

The incident became an important *cause celebre* in 1901 when a plebe who had been hazed unmercifully left West Point and died shortly afterwards. President McKinley ordered an investigation into the treatment of new cadets at the Academy. MacArthur, then a yearling, was summoned before the investigating committee and questioned closely about his own hazing.

Under oath, Doug avoided giving false testimony but tried to minimize his ordeal as much as possible, to protect the good name of the Academy. He also avoided naming three of the cadets who had hazed him because they were still enrolled, but named Barry and two others who had already been expelled.

The probers persisted in trying to get MacArthur to admit that hazing was a barbaric system. One official asked him, "Didn't you consider it cruel at that time?"

"I would like to have you define cruel," Doug hedged. When the dictionary definition was read to him, he admitted reluctantly, "I should say *perhaps* it was cruel, then."

Privately, he had no doubts about it at all. Throughout his career at the Academy he refused to take part in the hazing of any other cadets. He also preferred to look the other way rather than see rule violations which, if reported by a cadet on duty, would result in severe punishment for the offenders.

In September of Doug's plebe year, when cadets moved from tent camp to barracks, he was singled out for a unique honor. Arthur Hyde, a first-classman, sensed in him the potential of future greatness and invited MacArthur to share his rooms. The flattered cadet ran all the way to the West Point Hotel to consult his mother, who advised him to accept. Lights out in first-classmen's rooms didn't come until 11:00 p.m., two hours later than for plebes. "You'll have two hours longer to study every day," his mother pointed out shrewdly.

Doug not only used those two extra hours just that way, but also was up an hour before reveille every morning, poring over his books. He had a burning ambition to lead his class all the way through the Academy. "If I can graduate at the top of my class," he told Hyde candidly, "I'll have a chance to go up the military ladder even faster than my father. Do you know what I plan to be? Don't laugh, Arthur, because I'm in dead earnest— Chief of Staff of the United States Army!"

Even in those early days Doug MacArthur inspired fierce emotions in those around him, from loyal friends who applauded his high goals and brilliant talents to sarcastic enemies who conceded his abilities but deplored his ambitions as insufferable and vainglorious. One classmate remarked acidly, "He was arrogant from the age of eight." Another said, "To know MacArthur is to love him or to hate him. You can't just like him!"

MacArthur's career would have been less stormy if he had tried to cultivate the "common touch" like a later West Pointer, Dwight D. Eisenhower. Doug's crime was not so much in being the exceptional man as in knowing that he was. He refused to bid for popularity by disguising his ambition with false modesty. And he was often indiscreet enough to blurt out blunt truths he believed, regardless of the high-placed toes he trod upon in doing so.

His steadfast devotion to principle won him the approval of the most important person in his life, with whom he walked for half an hour every evening after supper, weather permitting. He was not allowed to visit his mother in her hotel, which was out of bounds for all cadets. Once he broke this rule and was sitting in her parlor with a cadet friend, George Cocheu, when a bellboy breathlessly broke in to warn them that the Academy Superintendent was on the way up to pay Mrs. MacArthur a call.

The boys dashed down a back stairway leading to the hotel cellar. Then George groaned, "There's no door leading outa here!" Doug studied the *cul-de-sac* swiftly, and made the kind of audacious decision which was so often to get him out of tight spots in Europe and the Pacific in the years ahead.

"Up the coal chute!" he barked. Disregarding his spotless gray uniform, he scrambled up the blackened chute and out a casement window as George followed hastily. Looking like mud-smeared commandos, the two cadets managed to sneak past the camp guard without being caught.

The "Salt Creek Club" was a clique of self-styled roughnecks led by Hugh "Iron Pants" Johnson, who later became a brigadier general and head of the celebrated N.R.A. under Roosevelt's New Deal. One day Johnson, then an upper-classman, confronted Doug at the head of his coterie.

"Mister MacArthur," Johnson growled in his sandpaper voice, "the Salt Creek Club takes a dim view of your unsportsmanlike efforts to excel everyone else at the Academy. Are you trying to impress Papa by becoming the Superintendent of West Point?"

Doug folded his arms, at the same time eyeing Johnson coolly. Instinct and military training told him not to be defensive, but to surprise the enemy with an improvised counter-attack. "Mr. Johnson," he said evenly, "you've guessed my intention very shrewdly. I *do* intend to be the head of the Academy one day—I can't think of a higher goal to aim at. But I promise you one thing. If your son should apply for West Point when I am its Superintendent, I will not hold it against him that Iron Pants Johnson was his father!"

There could be only one answer. The two boys retired to a remote area of the West Point athletic field and stripped off their shirts. Johnson, ten pounds heavier with powerful biceps, sought to make the battle a slugging match, but Doug's superior boxing skill sent his head snapping back with stinging jabs. The fight went on and on, each boy growing steadily wearier, with Johnson unable to land a punch solid enough to knock Doug off his feet, and MacArthur unable to wear away the bull-like strength of his aggressive opponent. Johnson finally grinned, stopped fighting, and grabbed Doug in a rough bear-hug.

"You're all right, kid," he panted hoarsely. "Plenty of guts! I guess we had you tagged as just a grind." He held out his hand and Doug shook it in weary relief. Soon after Johnson was referring to MacArthur as "the handsomest young man I've ever seen—brilliant, absolutely fearless." Doug's reputation soared further as shortstop on the Army's first baseball team, when he scored the winning run in a 4 to 3 victory over Navy. Although he was too light to make the football team, he nevertheless became team manager in his last year.

A number of pretty girls were escorted by Doug along the Academy's Flirtation Walk, where they gladly paused beneath Kissing Rock out of respect for the tradition that decreed: "If a cadet passes beneath with his best girl, and kisses her not, the rock will fall and crush them both." Rumor had it that the handsome cadet held an Academy record for being engaged to eight girls simultaneously. Pressed to confirm this years later, Doug would only say solemnly, "I do not recall being so heavily engaged by the enemy."

All too human, the pride of the Point collected his share of black marks on the "skin sheets" with crimes that included being short a pair of socks, having an unfluffed pillow at inspection, swinging his arms too much on parade, misspelling a word in an official communication, having long hair at inspection, and "trifling with drawn sabre in area, 11:06 a.m."

But his masterpiece of misbehavior escaped the skin sheets. One morning the Academy enjoyed some extra moments in bed because dawn's early light found the reveille cannon missing. Officers finally discovered it on a dormitory roof, where Doug and some friends had raised it after midnight with a carefully oiled derrick. It took the whole football squad to get it down again.

In the summer of 1901 Doug's father finally returned from the Philippines, and there was a happy family reunion in Milwaukee. Doug listened in fascination to his father's firsthand report of a feud with Judge (later President) William Howard Taft who, as the civil governor in Manila, had sent MacArthur Senior home for refusing to certify that a Filipino rebel army had been crushed when, in fact, it was still fighting. Indignant at this injustice, Doug silently vowed to avenge his father if the opportunity ever came his way.

At the end of his third year at the Academy, he was again awarded the highest military honor of the class by being named first captain—an honor that had gone to Robert E. Lee in 1828 and John J. Pershing in 1885. Giving up sports in his final year to fight for first place on the graduation list, Doug studied so relentlessly that he developed eye trouble and had to be hospitalized. He missed a math exam and found that his name had been posted on a list of "goats" who would have to take a special make-up exam because they were not doing well.

He burst out of the hospital, went directly to the home of the head math professor, and pounded stubbornly on the door until it was opened. "Sir," he declared, "I do not belong on the goat list. Unless my name is removed from it before classes tomorrow morning, I intend to resign from the Academy!"

He spent a bad night worrying how he could justify his rash act to his parents, with graduation only weeks away. But in the morning, to his utter relief, his name had disappeared from the offensive goat list.

Graduation Day was June 11, 1903. Doug, with a four-year average of 98.14, had made the best scholastic record in 101 years of West Point history, and also held the highest student military rank of first captain. No other cadet before Doug MacArthur had ever graduated with both academic and military top honors. He was now head of the student body, class salutatorian, and the cadet voted by his class as most likely to succeed. There were those who still resented him as holding too high an opinion of himself, while there were others who felt that for MacArthur to be modest would be hypocritical.

At the graduation ceremony Doug's parents were invited to sit on the platform with other notables, but they preferred to sit in the rear of the auditorium, possibly because the diplomas were being awarded by Howard Taft, now Secretary of War. General MacArthur had not forgotten or forgiven the indignity he had suffered at Taft's hands in Manila—and neither had Doug. Taft announced that MacArthur was the outstanding man of his class and called him to the platform. Doug marched up, saluted stiffly and accepted his diploma to an outburst of enthusiastic applause. But when the man who was to become President six years later extended his hand, Doug ignored it and saluted coldly instead. Facing about smartly, he walked straight to where his father sat, handed him the diploma, and sat down at his feet. It was a small yet proud gesture, and one not lost on Secretary Taft, who flushed an angry crimson.

No one appreciated the role that West Point played in his military career more than MacArthur himself. Even half a century later, weighed down by the highest honors that the nations of the world could bestow upon him, he looked back upon his graduation as a cadet as the proudest event of his whole life.

"Nearly forty-eight years have gone since I joined the long gray line," he reminisced from Tokyo. "As an Army 'brat' it was the fulfillment of all my boyish dreams. The world has turned over many times since that day and the dreams have long vanished with the passing years, but through the grim murk of it all, the pride and thrill of being a West Pointer has never dimmed. And as I near the end of the road, what I felt when I was sworn in on the Plain so long ago I can still say—'that is my greatest honor.'"

Less than ninety days after the bars of a second lieutenant were pinned on his shoulders, Doug sailed for the Philippines and his baptism of fire.

3
Young Hero in a Hurry

Promotions were swiftest in the Corps of Engineers, and the best place to get into action as soon as possible was the Philippines, so Doug chose them both. The islands were still in a state of turbulence with savage, bolo-swinging Moros fighting a guerilla war to drive the American occupation forces under Captain John J. ("Black Jack") Pershing into the sea.

The ambitious new second lieutenant, not yet twenty-four, was put to work cutting roads through Moro-infested bamboo and banyan jungles, and building wharves and piers to accommodate the shipping that could bring the Philippines into the twentieth century.

Doug found himself keenly exhilarated by his first overseas adventure in beautiful tropical islands. His senses delighted in the thick jungles, the rice terraces that furrowed the brows of volcanic mountains, the dreaming lakes, the pale blue and lacy white lagoons, the rich spice scents so unmistakably alien to American nostrils. It was the beginning of a lifelong love affair between Doug MacArthur and the Philippines.

He was touched, too, by the generous and warm hospitality of the Filipinos, who could not do enough for the son of the American general who had given them their first schools, hospitals, roads, and civil rights. This gratitude was not shared by the fierce Moros, fanatical native Moslems who believed that the only good Christian was a dead one.

MacArthur received his baptism of fire in October 1903, when he was sent to the island of Samar to clear jungles where no white man had dared tread before. While the 3rd Battalion of Engineers set to work, Doug led a patrol to flush out any Moros lying in ambush. With his .38 caliber service pistol in hand, he stalked through the heavily tangled undergrowth as silently as possible, trying to apply Indian tricks his father had taught him in the old days out West.

There was a sudden burst of shotgun fire from the thickets at one side of the patrol. MacArthur's orderly crumpled to the wet, steamy earth, his face half shot away. Doug dropped quickly beside him to render what aid he could. It was a fortunate impulse because a second blast roared out of the thickets, aimed at Doug's heart. It ripped off his campaign hat instead, and the patrolling Americans flung themselves to the soggy ground to fight off their hidden attackers.

A tough top sergeant handed MacArthur his shot-riddled hat and observed dryly, "With the Lieutenant's kind permission, may I remark that the rest of the Lieutenant's life is now on velvet?"

Doug grinned cockily. "Sergeant, don't you know that the fighting MacArthurs refuse to die any place but in bed?"

Not too long afterwards, while he was on another patrol, a short, stocky, brown-skinned Moro suddenly charged at him from ambush, swinging a razor-sharp bolo. MacArthur's .38 flipped into his hand and he emptied its chambers at his attacker. As the roar of the shots throbbed through the jungle, the Moro continued his deadly plunge. He fell two yards from Doug, his fierce bolo almost touching the American's boots.

Examining the dead tribesman, MacArthur found that each of his six expert shots had penetrated the Moro's heart. Yet the native had refused to stop until death had stilled his body. Doug was deeply impressed by this evidence of the Filipino's fanatical courage as a guerilla. He was to count heavily on this quality of the natives' fighting spirit in the dark and terrible days following Pearl Harbor.

At the end of a year in the Philippines MacArthur had distinguished himself well enough to be examined for promotion by the Manila Promotion Board. The officer serving as chairman posed a military problem impossible to solve, just to test Doug's ingenuity in trying to solve it. "MacArthur, how would you defend a harbor with a handful of men and little equipment, with just a few hours before the enemy comes at you over the ridges, and his fleet sails into the mouth of the harbor?"

Doug thought swiftly. "Well, sir, first I'd round up all the sign painters in the area to paint signs reading DANGER—HARBOR MINED. Then I'd float them out to the harbor entrance. After that I'd get down on my knees and pray. Then I'd go out with my men and fight like a tiger."

The bar on MacArthur's shoulders was silver when he sailed back to San Francisco. He knew it would not be long before he would return across the Pacific again, because the lure of the Islands was in his blood, and it thrilled him to feel part of the new adventure to build an outpost of American influence in the Western Pacific, just as his father had been a fighting part of opening up the American West in pioneering Army posts.

His opportunity came sooner than he expected. In 1905 war broke out between Russia and Japan. President Theodore Roosevelt, suspicious of Japan's imperialistic designs in the Pacific, decided he wanted a firsthand appraisal of the Japanese war machine in action. He despatched General Arthur MacArthur as chief American military observer with the Japanese forces fighting the Russians in Manchuria. Doug was appointed his father's aide-de-camp. One concern was uppermost in the minds of both father and son: were the Philippines in danger from the Japs?

Doug was greatly impressed by the fanaticism of Japanese troops in battle. He watched a thousand of them fall on their swords at the battle of the Yalu River, because Japanese headquarters had ordered them to fall back from pursuit of the Russians across the river, and they assumed that the order was issued because they had disgraced themselves in battle.

The Russians were no match for the Japanese war machine which steadily ground them to pieces. The climax of the war came when the Nipponese stood at the gates of Mukden. Doug watched the Japanese make a daring but desperate attack up a strategically vital hill strongly held by the Russians. They charged six times, but each time were driven off with severe losses.

Doug couldn't stand the role of innocent bystander any longer. Before his father could stop him, he impulsively raced across the field, consulted with the Japanese commander, then led a seventh charge up the hill. Impressed with his daring feat, the Jap infantry followed the lanky American all the way to the top of the hill and over it into the Russian trenches. After fierce hand-to-hand fighting, the Russians fled in a disorderly rout. The Battle of Mukden crowned the Japanese as the victors.

In their jubilation, Nipponese militarists told their troops, "The Orient shall be ruled by the Son of Heaven." MacArthur Senior reported to Washington that he was convinced the Japs had definite plans to conquer all of Asia and the Pacific, with later designs on Alaska and the west coast of the United States.

President Theodore Roosevelt ordered the MacArthurs on a secret mission around Asia, to sound out the military leaders of Hong Kong, Singapore, Siam, Java, the Malay States, Burma, Ceylon, and India on the possibility of common defense plans in the event of Japanese military aggression southward. It was a fascinating tour for Doug, deepening his insight into Asiatic thinking, and making him aware of the storms brewing in the Pacific.

"I don't think white colonialism can hold on much longer in Asia," Doug said to his father. "Do you?"

"No, it's just a matter of time. The big question is—will these small nations be able to stay free and independent, or will they be swallowed up by Japan or Russia?"

"I think that will probably depend on us, Governor. And the key to the whole thing is the Philippines. All of Asia will be watching what we do there, to see if we'll really help them without exploiting them, if we'll give them their independence when they're ready for it, and if we'll help them fight off any attempt by the Japs to invade them."

General MacArthur nodded. "That's about the size of it, Doug. But are Americans willing to fight to defend the Philippines if they have to? Do they understand that if the Japs are allowed to swallow the islands, they will swallow the rest of Asia, and then America would have to fight for its life?"

"Maybe we'd better do a little yelling when we get back, Governor, to wake them up and make them realize they've got a tiger loose in the back yard!"

Two years later, in a speech at the Old Settlers Club in San Francisco on February 22, 1908, Doug MacArthur sounded this warning: "It will be impossible for Americans to keep control of the Pacific unless we meet quickly the desperate attack which the Empire of Japan is at this very moment organizing against us."

But it took another thirty-three years before the terrible truth of this warning became clear to Americans in the columns of flame and black smoke charring the sky over Pearl Harbor.

When Doug returned to Washington with his father in 1906, he was thrilled to be taken to the White House to meet President Theodore Roosevelt. But an even greater thrill was in store for the handsome first lieutenant. While listening to the MacArthurs report personally on their nine-month tour of Asia, the President's piercing glance was largely fixed on the younger MacArthur, who sat as proudly as he stood. When it was time to say goodbye, Doug's handshake was as firm and muscular as Roosevelt's own.

"Douglas," the President growled, "how would you like to serve as my military aide in the White House?"

Any other twenty-six-year-old junior officer would have been rendered speechless by the unexpected honor. Doug, showing no surprise, asked, "When would you like me to start, Mr. President?"

Roosevelt's eyes twinkled. "In five minutes?"

"I won't need all that time, sir." Doug braced and saluted sharply. "Lieutenant MacArthur reporting for duty, Mr. President!"

Early in 1907 Doug demonstrated a flair for tactical strategy that delighted Roosevelt. A secret meeting of the cabinet had been called to discuss the financial panic agitating the country. Word of the conference leaked out, and Congressmen and newspapermen hurried to the White House. When Roosevelt came out of the conference room, they besieged him with questions.

The President's teeth clicked as they always did when he began to seethe with rage. MacArthur, standing at his side, tried to think of some way to head off an executive explosion. Suddenly he noticed a servant approaching with a tray of refreshments. Staring innocently at the ceiling, Doug thrust his foot out in the path of the servant, whose vision was blocked by the tray. There was a tremendous crash and splash as Congressmen and journalists scrambled frantically out of the way. No longer hemmed in, Roosevelt swiftly slipped back into the conference room and stayed there until the corridors had been cleared.

"Sorry I was so clumsy, Mr. President," Doug said dryly.

"Mac, you're a great diplomat," Roosevelt chuckled. "You ought to be an ambassador!"

When General Arthur MacArthur was promoted to the rank of lieutenant general, Doug was proudly certain that his father was going to be named the next Army Chief of Staff. But an ill wind blew in from the Philippines in the shape of his father's old enemy, Governor Taft, who returned from the islands to become Roosevelt's Secretary of War. Taft lost no time in humiliating General MacArthur by appointing one of his former aides instead.

Deeply offended, MacArthur Senior wrote Taft asking permission to retire from active service. When Taft granted this request promptly, General MacArthur left for his home in Milwaukee. Doug was heartbroken over his father's humiliation, and felt an overwhelming need to be close to him at this time. Turning his back on the White House and ignoring other important posts that could be his for the asking, Doug asked only to be assigned to the Army Engineering Office in Milwaukee so that he could live at home with his parents for awhile.

Doug could not conceal his bitterness. "It isn't fair!" he fumed to his father. "No man in the Army has done more for his country than you have. Why should the petty spite of a bureaucrat be allowed to deny you your just reward?"

"Son," General MacArthur said quietly, "I won't deny it hurts to be passed over. But I didn't become a soldier for rewards, promotions, or medals. No one can take away my real reward—the memories I have of serving my country."

"Honors belong to those who have earned them," Doug insisted stubbornly. "Right is right!"

A firm believer in justice, Doug never hesitated to give the devil his due, or to demand what he thought was right. His tenacious devotion to "the right thing," without regard for whose toes he trod upon, often made him seem coldly proud and arrogant. He never lacked for enemies, nor did he hesitate to make them among his superior officers if he believed them wrong.

When he angered the major in charge of the Army Engineering Office in Milwaukee, he was transferred to Fort Leavenworth along with a spiteful memo to the effect that he was "lacking in zeal to learn." He was nevertheless appointed an instructor to the post's Army Staff College, teaching majors, colonels, and even generals. These older officers were full of resentment at taking instruction from a twenty-nine-year-old first lieutenant, and threw questions at him designed to expose his ignorance. His ego took a merciless beating from his first class.

MacArthur adroitly devised a new strategy to cope with the problem for the next semester. He concluded his first lecture by remarking dryly, "Now, gentlemen, it is time for the question period. This is the opportunity for lazy students who need the instructor to think for them, or for apple-polishers seeking to flatter me, or for jackasses who want to embarrass me. Any questions?" There were no questions.

Another ingenious notion added to his reputation for tactical brilliance. The Fort's baseball team had lost every game they played against the local Kansas City Country Club nine until Doug took over as manager and outfielder. With the annual big game scheduled for 2:00 p.m., he invited the enemy to a luncheon banquet of hot dogs, baked beans, hamburgers, pigs knuckles, sauerkraut, corn on the cob, and beer. When the bloated Kansans waddled out on the diamond, they met their first defeat at the hands of the MacArthur nine, who banqueted *afterwards*.

In 1912, when Doug had been made a captain, shocking news came in a telegram from Milwaukee. His father, guest of honor at a 50th reunion of the ninety survivors of the 24th Wisconsin Infantry, had suddenly keeled over and died of a stroke in the midst of a speech recalling the dimmed glories of the Civil War.

Rushing home on emergency leave, Doug found his brother Arthur, who was now a lieutenant commander in the Navy, already there. Together they did their best to console their mother; she found it difficult to believe that the indomitable husband who had escaped death dozens of times was finally lost to her. The shock had forced her to take to bed.

Arthur showed Doug a telegram that had just reached him from the Secretary of the Navy, advising Arthur that his destroyer had won the official pennant of the entire Navy. "It came too late, Doug," he muttered unhappily. "If only I could have shown this to the Governor before he went!"

"He didn't need that to be proud of you, Art," Doug said.

"It might have helped him forgive me for choosing the Navy instead of the Army, like you. Doug, what are we going to do about Mother? She'll need one of us to look after her now."

"I know. Army rules won't let her live with me at Fort Leavenworth. So I'm asking for a transfer to the Office of the Chief of Engineers in Washington. I'll take her with me."

One fact about his father's burial made a deep impression upon Doug. It was a civilian funeral because a few days before General MacArthur's death he had said to his wife, "When I die bury me in civilian dress. I have worn the uniform nearly all my life—let me rest in peace as an American citizen." To Doug this was a new image of his father he had not really suspected . . . a tired man for whom civilian peace had come to mean more than military glory. Doug wondered if the arts of war would ever lose their savor for him, too.

His transfer came through, and he and his mother kept house together in a modest Washington apartment. Mrs. MacArthur made a slow recovery, and Doug spent as much time at home with her as he could. They had only been in Washington for four weeks when MacArthur's career suddenly took a giant leap forward. He had come to the attention of Major General Leonard Wood, who was now Army Chief of Staff. Wood made inquiries about Doug and learned that the handsome young captain not only had a remarkable grasp of war tactics and strategy, but was also a man of integrity, fearless in disagreeing with his superiors if he believed that they were wrong and he was right.

Wood appointed him to the General Staff, the brains of the Army, which had only thirty-eight officers. The fact that MacArthur at thirty-two was the youngest of them all did not deter him from filing one-man minority reports challenging majority opinions with which he could not agree. Generals were often vexed to find that after long hours of study, they came up with the same answers to a problem that Doug had reached swiftly by brilliant intuition. General Wood frequently acted on MacArthur's views.

"I think the generals would court-martial me in a minute," Doug admitted ruefully to his mother, "if it wasn't for General Wood."

His mother handed him a cup of tea. "Your father used to say that the higher a man's star rises, the more of a target he becomes. But if his star is a true one, it can't be brought down."

Her words found an echo in his heart, and he threw her a grateful glance. "Yes, but to insist on the truth, and make it stick, you need *four* true stars. Here. . . ." He touched his shoulder. "And I intend to have them!"

4
One-Man Invasion of Mexico

Leading the serene, pressed-pants existence of a typical junior officer of the Army General Staff in Washington, Doug found himself growing restless, eager to prove himself in the field. It meant little to him at first when General Victoriano Huerta began shooting his way to power in Mexico. But trouble brewed swiftly when the new Huerta government began arresting Americans illegally, and its officials offered studied insults to the United States Government.

After several provocative incidents, President Wilson sent a US naval force to blockade the Mexican port of Vera Cruz, and Marines landed on April 21, 1914. The Marines fought a brief but bloody battle with Mexican troops, seizing the Vera Cruz customs house and holding it. War fever mounted in the United States, fanned by jingoistic newspapers and oil companies worried about Mexican investments. The uproar prodded the US Army General Staff into sending an expeditionary force to Vera Cruz . . . just in case. Then, on April 22nd Major General Leonard Wood, Army Chief of Staff, called on Secretary of War Lindley M. Garrison.

"I want permission to send a reconnaissance mission into Mexico," he told Garrison. "If this thing erupts into a real war, we'll need to know the lay of the land beyond Vera Cruz."

"It's risky," the Secretary of War frowned. "What if they get caught? Wilson doesn't want us to do anything that might rock the boat, as long as there's a chance to negotiate."

"I only need to send one man, and I promise you he won't get caught. Captain Douglas MacArthur is a highly resourceful and daring man—one of my best junior officers."

On May 1st when the battleship *Nebraska* sailed into the azure waters of Vera Cruz, Doug MacArthur came ashore in the first launch. His credentials, presented to General Funston, simply stated that he was an "unattached and independent agent of the General Staff and War Department, to be allowed complete freedom of movement."

MacArthur attempted to ascertain how American troops would be able to move inland from Vera Cruz if the order came to fight. An old infantry friend, Captain Constant Cordier, told him that the advance would have to be a painfully slow one on foot because there were no locomotives on the trains captured in Vera Cruz. When fighting had broken out at the port, the Mexicans had unhitched the engines and driven them off to some hiding place.

At a native bar in a narrow, cobbled street behind Vera Cruz's palm-lined boulevard, Doug located a Mexican engineer who had driven for the Vera Cruz and Alvarado Railroad before it had suspended operations. Miguel Cardenas y Perote, a husky Mexican with a fierce mustache, told him that the engines were hidden somewhere on the line between Vera Cruz and Alvarado, but he didn't know exactly where.

"I'll pay you a hundred dollars to help me locate them."

Miguel tugged uneasily at a soiled collar. "Lots of patrols around, *senor,* and *bandidos.* If they catch me with a *gringo* soldier . . ." He drew his finger across his neck.

"We'd leave when it gets dark and be back before dawn." Doug studied the hesitant Mexican. "One hundred fifty dollars?"

They settled for two hundred in gold when Miguel explained they would need two more men to meet them halfway on the line with a narrow gauge handcar. The wide gauge Isthmus line did not go directly to Alvarado but was met halfway by a narrow gauge line at Paso del Toro.

"Let me go with you, Doug," Cordier pleaded. "Suppose this Mexican leads you into a bandit trap? Or tips off the Mexican Army? Or tries to kill you to rob you?"

MacArthur grinned. "You mean a soldier can get hurt?"

On the evening of May 9, 1914, with threatening black clouds scudding low in the sky, two men worked vigorously at the tandem drive shaft of a rusty handcar. It rolled along unweeded tracks leading to Boca del Rio, a sleepy little town on the east bank of the Jamapa River.

"We take rowboat here, *senor*. The bridge, she is down."

Doug mopped his dripping face with the sleeve of his soaked uniform and jumped down, his identification tags clinking around his neck. Straining and grunting, he helped Miguel lift the vehicle off the rails, push it to the edge of a nearby coffee plantation, and conceal it behind thick foliage.

Miguel led the way to a rowboat hidden near the shattered bridge, which had been blown up by Mexican troops. They rowed diagonally downstream, landing on the opposite side well below the lighted lanterns of Boca del Rio. Two tethered ponies were waiting for them behind a deserted shack. Detouring around the town, they rode to the rendezvous point where two Mexican firemen were waiting for them on the narrow gauge line with another handcar.

Miguel hid the ponies and the four men rolled south. Each time their handcar approached a town, MacArthur ordered a halt and he and Miguel leaped off. Lashing their wrists together to prevent separation in the dark, Doug detoured around town through the woods. The two firemen pumped the handcar through the town to pick them up half a mile south.

"You say we must hurry," panted Miguel. "But we waste all this time running around the villages!"

"No one must report a Yankee uniform this far inside Mexico." Mopping his face, MacArthur wrung out his handkerchief.

"Then why did you wear it, *senor?*"

"Because I'm a soldier, my friend, not a spy."

One hour after midnight they approached Alvarado.

"Senor Capitan—look!" Miguel's voice shook with excitement and he flung out a pudgy arm. Peering through the gloom, Doug dimly made out the massive outlines of five locomotives off on a spur track to the left. He leaped from the handcar even before it had slowed to a halt, and Miguel jumped heavily after him. They scrambled up and through one locomotive after another.

"Two are switch engines," Miguel reported. "No good for what you need, *senor.* But three are fine road pullers."

"What shape are they in?"

"They will run. Just a few small parts are missing."

"Can you get replacements?"

"For a few more gold pieces, *si, senor!'*

Exultant, MacArthur made a few map notations by carefully shielded matchlight, then scrambled down from the last engine and trotted back toward the handcar with Miguel at his heels. The firemen pumped them back toward Paso del Toro.

Just before Salinas, Doug took his usual precaution of circling the town on foot with Miguel tied to his wrist. They had not gone far when they heard guttural voices and harsh laughter in a grove about one hundred yards to their right.

"Bandidos, senor!" Miguel whispered hoarsely.

The long legs of Doug MacArthur broke their stride, and his abrupt halt almost spilled the Mexican. They peered through the heavy foliage, which gave off an almost overpowering smell of wild tropical flowers, but the night was too dark to see well.

Then Miguel held up five trembling fingers and Doug nodded grimly. He knew he could expect no mercy from a guerilla band because while Mexican troops took prisoners, bandits did not.

"They are coming this way, *Senor Capitan!*"

MacArthur slid his automatic out of his holster and released the safety. "We'll have to make a run for it. Can you keep up?"

"I do not know, *senor.* You are so long in the leg!"

"Come on!" The two men bolted through the underbrush like quail flushed out of a reedy swamp. Doug plunged forward as fast as Miguel's heavy weight would allow him, startling the bandits who opened fire and began pursuit. Dragging his human anchor, MacArthur ran toward a clearing where a narrow dirt road wound toward the railroad line as it emerged out of Salinas.

The stocky Mexican's feet suddenly shot out from under him and he went sprawling headfirst into the dirt. Doug found himself yanked violently backward as the earth rose to crash against him.

Rolling on his side, he leveled his automatic as flashes of yellow light stabbed the night. Dirt spewed into his face as a bullet dug into the road inches in front of him, but he held his fire, waiting for a sharp target. A burly bandit came running over rising ground, silhouetted against the night sky. He saw them and fired just as Doug squeezed off a carefully-aimed shot. The bandit spun around, falling against a tree.

MacArthur didn't wait for the other desperadoes to catch up. Springing to his feet, he jerked Miguel up with him and the two men raced down the road.

They heard the iron wheels, and the handcar loomed up in the darkness. Slowing to let the two wrist-bound men scramble aboard, it rolled away from Salinas at top speed.

Just before Piedra, when MacArthur jumped off the handcar for another detour on foot with Miguel, the rain thickened, churning the ground and making the going slippery. A steamy fog rose from the earth, shrouding the path in front of them.

"Can you see where we're going, Miguel?"

"No, *senor.* We slow up, *si?*"

"No! Only a few hours left before daybreak!"

Without warning both men suddenly crashed into something that seemed at first like a wall of hot, hard flesh. The collision staggered them to one side, and through smoky wraiths they saw the rear flanks of a horse as it swerved backwards. In its saddle was a grim-faced Mexican with a rifle slung over his shoulder. Then Doug saw that he was one of a company of mounted men.

The guerillas were equally startled. Several began to yell, horses wheeled and collided in confusion, rifles were unslung, and began blazing in the fog. Trapped in the center of the melee, MacArthur was knocked off his feet by the rush of two horsemen in a collision so violent that he felt as though his neck had been broken. Miguel, yanked by their wrist bonds, was flung to the ground with him. Only the merciful darkness and the heavy fog saved both men from instant death.

Three bullets pierced Doug's uniform, grazing his ribs and hip, while a fourth ploughed into Miguel's right shoulder. In the chaos and shouting one bandit shot another in the foot and a second wild bullet brought down a horse. Taking advantage of the turmoil, MacArthur scrambled into foliage at the side of the road, jerking Miguel with him. The bandits, unsure where their prey had disappeared to, began firing at random into the thickets.

Flattening himself behind a low rock, Doug took out his automatic and waited patiently for targets. As he squeezed off four careful shots, three bandits crashed off their mounts, one after the other. The other guerillas, suddenly realizing that they were silhouetted for a hidden gun in ambush, prudently spurred their horses and galloped off toward Piedra.

"Please, *senor!*" Miguel groaned in agony. "Do not make me to get off the handcar any more!"

"Are you hit?"

"*Si*. In the shoulder."

Working in the dark, MacArthur ripped the Mexican's shirt where he felt it saturated and sticky. Tearing off his own sweat-soaked undershirt, he bound the wound tightly to staunch the blood. His own wound, he noted, was too superficial to worry about.

When they regained the handcar on the far side of Piedra, Doug kneeled to make his lap a pillow for the wounded man's head. Approaching Laguna, MacArthur decided that there was no help for it but to stay on the handcar as it clattered through town. At first the sleeping village seemed deserted, but then they heard galloping hooves.

"Faster!" MacArthur grated.

The gasping firemen redoubled their efforts as sporadic shots tore through the night in their direction. Doug fired back twice, then scrambled to his feet to join the Mexicans in making the handcar fairly fly along the rails. Two pursuing horsemen, outdistanced, fell back, but a third rider on a swift horse overtook and paced them. MacArthur glimpsed the sombrero of the Mexican Army as the galloping soldier fired pointblank.

A bullet ripped through the bottom of Doug's billowing shirt, a second pinged off the pumping bar an inch from his hand, and a third thudded into the car close to his foot. He let go the bar, turned, and fired twice. The soldier's horse neighed shrilly and stumbled, flinging its rider out of the saddle. The horse pitched across the tracks in front of the handcar, causing a violent collision that almost hurled the four men off.

The vehicle ground to a stop, its iron wheels mangling and dragging the dead beast. Doug sprang off the platform, pistol ready as he ran back toward the fallen soldier, but the man lay unconscious, his head against a fence post. MacArthur had aimed only at the horse, reluctant to kill a soldier who had simply been doing his duty for a country with which the United States was not actually at war.

The two firemen worked frantically to remove the animal's carcass from the wheels and track. "This night I will never forget!" Miguel groaned. "For three bags of gold, *senor*, I would not take such terrible chances again!"

But the night was not through with them yet. At Boca del Rio, after the firemen had left them and they were crossing the Jamapa River in the rowboat they had hidden, they struck a submerged tree. Violent currents pinned the boat against branches, pressure building up until it capsized, spilling the two men into fast-flowing water. Weary from the long ordeal, Doug felt the churning waters suck him under and fought to keep his head above the torrents.

He struggled until he could touch river bottom, then gratefully pulled himself ashore. As he turned, he saw that Miguel was drowning, his bandaged arm and shorter stature making him helpless in the swirling waters. MacArthur took a deep breath and thrashed back into the churning water. Grabbing the Mexican, he turned him on his back and towed him laboriously to shore. Both men crawled out of the river thoroughly exhausted.

Perilously close to the end of his strength, Doug saw day faintly breaking in the east. His whole mission could be imperilled now by sunrise. But both men were so weak their legs would not carry them from the bank for another ten minutes. Then MacArthur croaked, "We've got to hurry!"

They finally staggered back to the edge of the coffee plantation and, with a last groaning effort, managed to drag the handcar they had hidden there back onto the tracks. Miguel could pump with only one arm. As both men toiled painfully, sick with the lack of sleep, the car rolled slowly back to the outskirts of Vera Cruz. It inched to a halt yards from where the adventure had begun about twelve hours before.

Doug half-fell to the ground, then helped Miguel down. Supporting each other, they lurched toward the sunlit city. MacArthur booked a room in a small Vera Cruz hotel, then sent word to Captain Cordier. An Army doctor, sworn to secrecy, arrived swiftly to attend to Miguel's shoulder wound. When the lanky American adventurer was assured that the wound was not infected, and that the Mexican engineer would be all right, he fell back on the bed and slept for fourteen straight hours. Miguel, a clean bandage on his wound, snored heavily in bed beside him.

General Leonard Wood, at Governor's Island preparing to take over the American expeditionary forces if war with Mexico should materialize, received a communication from Captain Cordier, written without Doug MacArthur's knowledge:

"I am taking the liberty of sending you this personal letter in order that a daring reconnaissance of Captain Douglas MacArthur, General Staff Corps, may properly be brought to your attention. In my opinion, his splendid and hazardous undertaking calls for the bestowal of a Medal of Honor. . . . It was a test of supreme courage; and in my opinion, it stands out boldly as the only distinguished exploit since the landing of our Army on Mexican soil. If any deed of daring merits the Medal of Honor, surely MacArthur's audacious undertaking is one."

When Doug returned to Washington he received an order from General Wood to write out a full report of the mission, which was then forwarded to the Adjutant General. Wood recommended that MacArthur be awarded the Medal of Honor for voluntarily performing "at the risk of his life a most gallant and hazardous act—an act calling for more than could reasonably be expected in the way of risk of life."

Meanwhile the Mexican crisis had blown over, and Major General Funston returned to Galveston. He agreed that MacArthur did, indeed, deserve the Medal, but how could *he* recommend it when he'd been kept ignorant of the mission—when, in fact, it violated his own orders from the Secretary of War to avoid all possible risks of provoking Mexico to war?

Funston's own aide-de-camp, however, reported that Doug had turned over to him the intelligence about the locomotives, and that this had become the foundation of their plans: "Our first aggressive steps would have been to seize the engines that Captain MacArthur located, and thus make it possible to supply the column when it advanced. The practical importance of this information, if we had moved into Mexico, cannot be overestimated. I am thoroughly familiar with all the conditions surrounding the reconnaissance, and unhesitatingly pronounce it one of the most dangerous and difficult feats in Army annals."

However a reviewing board of three officers coolly rejected the recommendation. True, MacArthur *had* been daring and ingenious, but he had been most unwise in undertaking such a politically delicate adventure without General Funston's knowledge. If they gave him a Medal of Honor for exceeding his authority, other officers might be similarly tempted in the hope of glory.

Doug was furious. Not being awarded the Medal of Honor was one thing, but being rapped over the knuckles for heroism was another. Rashly he went over the heads of the board and protested to the Chief of Staff himself that the verdict was both unfair and unjustly humiliating. This bold action by a mere captain raised eyebrows in high places. Army discipline required that MacArthur's appeal be summarily rejected, especially since he had violated the chain of command. This arrogant firebrand, the brass agreed privately, would have to be cut down to size.

5

D'Artagnan of the Western Front

In 1916 the ominous thunder of Europeans at war rolled across the Atlantic toward a neutral America. The new US Secretary of War, Newton D. Baker, was convinced that the nation had to be won over to a policy of national preparedness. To persuade Americans to the War Department's views, he chose Major Douglas MacArthur as his Chief of Press Relations. In this capacity Doug became a colleague and good friend of the Assistant Secretary of the Navy, Franklin Delano Roosevelt.

MacArthur's skillful work with America's press helped arouse growing indignation against Germany's unrestricted submarine warfare, and prepared the way for America's entrance into the war on the side of the Allies—Britain, France, Russia and Italy—and against the Central Powers—Germany, Austria-Hungary, Turkey and Bulgaria—in March, 1917.

Doug eagerly sought to escape his desk in Washington for action overseas. He proposed raising a fighting division out of National Guard units from each state. When the rest of the General Staff made it clear they considered the National Guard good for little but armory drills, MacArthur persuaded Baker to let him appeal directly to President Wilson, "A division containing National Guardsmen from every state in the union would stir national pride and enthusiasm, Mr. President," Doug urged, sweeping his arm in a dramatic arc. "It would stretch across the nation, from the Atlantic to the Pacific—like a great rainbow!"

Wilson toyed thoughtfully with his glasses. Then he turned to Baker and announced, "That's exactly what well call it—the Rainbow Division."

Officially designated as the 42nd Division, the Rainbow landed at St. Nazaire, France, on March 18th, with Colonel Douglas MacArthur as Chief of Staff to Commanding General William Mann. The colors of the Rainbow also embraced three other men destined to become famous—"Wild Bill" Donovan of the "Fighting 69th," most decorated hero of the A.E.F.; Father Francis Duffy, whose statue stands at the crossroads of the world in New York City's Times Square; and a flinty little Missourian in the field artillery, Captain Harry S. Truman, who thirty-four years later was ironically destined to end the military career of MacArthur.

Shortly after the 42nd's arrival on French soil, General Mann showed Doug an order from General John J. Pershing, Commander-in-Chief of the American Expeditionary Forces, stating that the Rainbow would not go into battle as a division, but would replace troops as needed in other divisions.

MacArthur was furious. "He can't do this to the Rainbow!"

"Old Black Jack," Mann sighed, "never changes his mind."

"Maybe Washington will change it for him!"

Avoiding military channels, Doug brashly sent a private cable back to Secretary of War Baker: PERSHING INTENDS CHOP UP RAINBOW FOR REPLACEMENTS STOP MEANS RUIN OF CRACK DIVISION TRAINED TO WORK AS TEAM AND DESTROY MORALE OF TROOPS PROUD OF BEING RAINBOW MEN STOP URGE PROMPT ACTION TO SAVE THE DIVISION SPONSORED BY PRESIDENT WILSON HIMSELF MACARTHUR.

Word of this temerity reached Pershing, who reacted with explosive indignation. He summoned MacArthur to A.E.F.

headquarters and roared, "How dare you—a mere colonel—sit in judgment on orders of the Supreme Commander?"

Doug's voice was clear and undaunted. "Sir, your order would not give you the fighting replacements you need, but only bitter men whose morale was destroyed when the Army broke its promise to let them fight under their own banner of the Rainbow!"

Pershing's outraged glare mirrored the autocratic, humorless mind behind it as he snapped ominously, "Young man, I do not like your attitude!"

Two days later the War Department informed Pershing that the Rainbow was to be left intact as a fighting unit. It was an unprecedented victory of a colonel over the commanding general of an entire army. Thereafter Pershing's eyes took on a steely glint at the mere mention of the name of MacArthur.

The replacement of General Mann by General Charles T. Menoher did not alter Doug's tactical command of the Rainbow. He trained his men to a fine edge in France's coldest winter of the century, putting himself through every hardship that he asked of his troops. On February 14, 1918, they were finally ordered to reinforce the French 7th Army Corps on the Lunéville Baccarat front, and were welcomed to the trenches with a deafening barrage of bursting shells and machine-gun fire.

To ease the tension of his green troops in their baptism under fire, MacArthur strolled casually through the trenches as though out for a Sunday walk in the park. Rainbow men were first startled, then cheered, at the sight of the tall, slender figure in pullover sweater, loose muffler, and riding breeches. Instead of a helmet Doug wore a battered overseas cap, and in place of a gas mask he carried a riding crop. A jeweled cigarette holder jutted between his teeth as he exchanged lighthearted greetings with all the doughboys he passed.

The French were completely baffled at the sight of a division's chief of staff who scorned the safety and comfort of the rear echelon for the filth, misery, and danger of the front. A French captain was even more astonished when MacArthur asked to join a reconnaissance raid he was making into German lines.

Shortly after midnight Doug smeared his face with mud and crawled out of the trench with the French patrol. German machine guns raked the desolate landscape, spurting plugs of mud in his eyes. A red flare burst overhead, eerily illuminating the crawling figures. They sprang to their feet, hurling grenades as they charged through a rain of bullets. Doug sprinted after them, lunging headlong on top of a German machine-gun nest.

In a few savage moments of hand-to-hand fighting, the Germans were killed and a number of raiders sprawled lifeless beside them. As more Germans came rushing up from trenches behind, the patrol sprinted back to their own lines. When the survivors leaped into the Allied trenches, Doug was not among them. Deep gloom settled among men of the Rainbow.

Then two dim figures were seen approaching the Allied lines, walking erect. One of them proved to be a Boche colonel with his hands up, being prodded forward by a riding crop in his back which he evidently mistook for a pistol. When Doug scrambled into the trench with his prisoner, doughboy merriment was doubled by the fact that their reckless colonel had left the seat of his pants behind on some barbed wire. Rainbow battle spirit soared proudly the following afternoon as the Croix de Guerre was pinned on their leader by order of General DeBazelaire.

Two weeks later at Reichicourt, Doug led two companies of Rainbow men on a large-scale French raid which brought back a thousand prisoners. His cool courage during this raid caused the French to cite him for gallantry in action. Early in March the French 7th Army Corps turned over the whole position to MacArthur's men. Doug was the first man over the top in an all-Rainbow attack against the heavily defended Bois des Feyes.

In the din of frightening explosions that chewed up running men and rancid earth, he heard a new sound that made his eyes snap warily—a low warning whistle followed by a dull thud but no explosion. Gas shells! He refused to turn back, although he was the only one among his men without a gas mask. Continuing to race forward at the head of the Rainbow, he stumbled into a pocket of mustard gas. His lungs felt as though they were on fire, and as he gasped for air his eyes began to burn so painfully that he was blinded. When he fell, he shook off the adjutant who sought to carry him off the battlefield.

"No!" he cried. "Not till we've taken the Bois!"

Only when the Germans had been routed did he allow himself to be carted off to a first aid tent. He refused to go to a field hospital in the rear, for fear of being separated from the Rainbow. He remained active at Division Headquarters even though he had to wear a blindfold for ten days, and suffered severely from gas poisoning.

"You're getting the Distinguished Service Cross, Mac," Menoher told him gruffly. "But I think you ought to know that a lot of top brass at G.H.Q. consider you irresponsible, and feel you have no business leading attacks like some expendable line officer!"

"General," Doug replied, "I don't consider line officers in the Rainbow any more expendable than I am. I lead them to prove it, and I think it makes for a fighting spirit. When I went over the top, I'll admit there were a dozen terrible seconds when I felt that they weren't following me. But then, without turning around, I knew how wrong I was to doubt them. In another moment they were all around me . . . and lots of them raced ahead of me!"

The men of the Rainbow began fondly referring to their dashing battle leader as "D'Artagnan of the Western Front," "Beau Brummell of the A.E.F." and "the Fighting Dude." At Pershing's headquarters, however, MacArthur was referred to by underrated staff officers as "the Showoff."

The beginning of spring, 1918, brought an all-out German offensive to take Paris before the full might of Pershing's new two-million-man American army could be brought to bear on the Western Front. For eighty-two straight days the Rainbow Division bore the brunt of the fierce front-line fighting. MacArthur's headquarters were never more than a thousand yards behind the most forward trench, but he was more often to be found crawling through the mud with some patrol.

When the Rainbow Division was relieved in the line on June 16th, more than two thousand of its men had been killed or wounded. But they had held fast against everything the crack German divisions of Ludendorff could throw at them. Marching sixty kilometers through the mud to the rear, the men of the 42nd were bone-weary, filthy, and bearded—but proud.

At Charmes they unexpectedly encountered General Pershing and some staff officers in a command car. The Supreme Commander professed to be aghast at the condition of the Rainbow's men and equipment. In front of everyone he turned on MacArthur and yelled, "This division is a disgrace! The whole outfit is just about the worst I have ever seen! They're an undisciplined, filthy rabble—a disgrace to the United States Army!"

Doug fought hard to hang on to his temper. "General, these men have just come off the line after eighty-two days—"

"Silence!" Pershing roared. "That's no excuse for failing to look or act like American soldiers! MacArthur, I'm going to hold you personally responsible for getting discipline and order into this division—or heaven help the whole pack of you!"

Despite Pershing's personal dislike of him, Doug's brilliance in the field was acknowledged by his promotion to the rank of brigadier general on June 26, 1918.

After fighting briefly on the Champagne front, the Rainbow was ordered to the Marne. Here they were under the tactical command of General Henri Gouraud of the 4th French Army, who told Menoher and MacArthur that the Germans were retreating from their positions on the Ourcq River. Gouraud ordered the 42nd to cross the Ourcq silently at dawn and turn the retreat into a rout with a surprise bayonet attack. Doug was surprised to hear that the Germans were abandoning such strong positions.

The enemy's "retreat" proved to be a ruse to lure the Allies into an unwary advance. After a long and bloody battle, the men of the Rainbow did drive the Germans back, but only by cleaning them out, a nest at a time, with hand grenades and heavy artillery support. The cost of this victory to the 42nd Division was appalling—six thousand casualties.

MacArthur was bitter. "It's my fault for having taken Gouraud's word for it that the Germans were retreating," he told his adjutant. "I *knew* it didn't make sense militarily. I should have trusted my own judgment. Never again will I let my men be sacrificed like that—not if I hang for it! From now on I'll make all my own reconnaissance personally."

He did exactly that shortly afterwards at the freshly captured town of Sergy, chasing after the retreating enemy on the running board of a speeding ambulance. What he saw convinced him that this was a real rout, and a golden opportunity. He rushed back to divisional headquarters and tried to talk Menoher into forging ahead after the disorganized Germans.

"Now? Mac, you're crazy! Every man in the Rainbow who isn't buried or wounded is dead on his feet. Besides, we've got no orders to advance." When Doug refused to take no for an answer, Menoher finally snapped, "All right, but you'll have to stick your own neck out. I can't give you written orders!"

"Good enough, General," Doug grinned. "Thanks!"

He raced around the division front, explaining to his exhausted men their chance to cripple the retreating German divisions by a fierce pursuit. Trusting Doug, inspired by his enthusiastic appeal, they whooped after him at the heels of the withdrawing enemy. Slashing the German rear severely, they strewed the field with enemy dead and equipment, stopping only when they had captured the main ridge of Nesselers Forest.

"MacArthur seems to be fighting his own personal war," Pershing grumbled. But he approved another medal for him. And Menoher let the maverick young general take over complete command of the Rainbow's 84th Infantry Brigade, to try out some new ideas MacArthur was developing about field command.

In September the Rainbow joined other American divisions on the St. Mihiel front. During an 8-day battle to dislodge the Germans from Metz, Doug was everywhere on the battlefield, never seeming to sleep, always encouraging his men, improvising orders as he advanced. His long woollen scarf, which had been knitted for him by his mother, flapped behind him on the windy battlefield like a banner.

Once, his headquarters' staff caught up with him long enough to join him for a meal. As they were seated at a table, a shell exploded, blowing to bits an orderly bringing food on a tray. Doug's officers dashed for shelter. In another moment they heard him call out cheerfully, "Come back with me, gentlemen—you're safer here. The Germans still haven't figured out how to make a shell that can kill me!" When they sheepishly returned to the table, he told them with deep conviction about the indestructibility of the MacArthur clan.

At the outskirts of Essey the slashing advance of the 84th Infantry was held up by the breakdown of American tanks. German shells and mortars ripped fluttering yellow slashes in the dark rain, forcing Doug's men to advance in the mud on their bellies. He strode around impatiently waiting for the tanks to catch up, and was joined by six officers in a command car, one of them being Colonel George S. Patton, Jr., commander of the US Tank Brigade. An enemy shell screamed toward them.

Patton's staff officers dived out of the car and hugged the earth. MacArthur and Patton—the only two high-ranking officers in the A.E.F. who led their own troops on the battle-field—stood erect, eyeing each other as the shell burst danger-ously close to their position. Patton flinched instinctively, then looked annoyed with himself. Doug grinned. "Don't worry, Colonel," he said dryly. "You never hear the one that gets you."

MacArthur was slightly wounded during the St. Mihiel offen-sive, but again refused to be hospitalized. He led the 84th Brigade in a breakthrough of German lines and speared toward Metz, which appeared to him open to easy capture. However, he was already far ahead of any other American troops, and he had strict orders from Supreme Headquarters not to advance any farther.

Unwilling to see so great a prize slip through his fingers, MacArthur left the 84th camped on hills above the vulnerable rail center and rushed back to Pershing's G.H.Q. He begged the wintry general to let him attack Metz, promising to take it in forty-eight hours. Carried away by his own enthusiasm, he added, "The President would certainly make you a field marshal for it, and I think you'll agree I would have earned a second star!"

"Get out!" Pershing roared in fury, "and stay out!"

"I made a mistake in timing," Doug told his adjutant. "I should have taken Metz and *then* asked his permission!"

The last great battle of the war began on September 25th, when a million American troops in twenty-seven divisions fought to smash the Hindenburg Line. On October 1st the Rainbow Divi-sion moved up to the Meuse-Argonne front, which the rainy season had churned into a sea of thick mud. MacArthur lost no time in making his own reconnaissance of the battlegrounds.

Returning, he was caught in another poison gas barrage and stumbled back to his headquarters severely injured, but as adamant as ever against hospitalization. Shortly afterward, however, he was wounded by an American shell fragment and fell unconscious. When he woke up he was in a field hospital, where he was firmly detained for almost a month. Ignoring the doctors' refusal to discharge him, Doug put on his battered cap and escaped back to his men.

One rainy, windswept night General Charles P. Summerall, commander of the Fifth Corps, suddenly appeared in the Rainbow's advance command post where MacArthur was studying field maps by candlelight. He told Doug that the American advance had bogged down because of a heavily fortified key hill in the Hindenburg Line, the Cote de Chatillon, which had resisted all attacks.

"Mac," Summerall said tersely as he sat down and took a sip of Doug's coffee, "you will give me Cote de Chatillon tomorrow or turn in a report of five thousand casualties."

Doug regarded him steadily. "This brigade will capture Cote de Chatillon tomorrow, sir, or you can report every man in it as a casualty. And at the top of the list will be the name of the brigade commander!"

The fortress-like hill bristled with barbed wire, machine guns, artillery, and crack German troops who could cover the hill with crossfire from trenches and concrete pillboxes. MacArthur ordered aerial reconnaissance photos to be made immediately. Poring over these with a magnifying glass, he uttered a cry of triumph as he discovered a small gap in the wire on one flank, where the posts had apparently been loosened by the heavy rain of the night before. That night Doug and his men crawled silently through this gap, their faces blackened with mud, using only bayonets and knives. Fanning out around the hill's trenches and machine-gun pits, they leaped steel-first down at the astonished enemy. Hand grenades flung through the slits of pillboxes turned them into cement coffins.

With incredibly light casualties for so important a victory, MacArthur's commandos planted the American flag and the regimental colors of the Rainbow on top of Cote de Chatillon. The Fifth Corps promptly roared through this vital crack in the Hindenburg Line, and the key to final victory had been turned.

General Menoher was moved up from the 42nd Division to head the Sixth Corps, and Doug became commander in name, as he had been in fact, of the entire Rainbow Division. It was a signal honor for a young brigadier general of only thirty-eight.

In the last days of the war the daredevil commander was finally taken prisoner—but not by the enemy. On November 6th he had been making a two-man reconnaissance with Major Walter B. Wolf, his chief of staff, when they were suddenly surrounded by a patrol of trigger-happy doughboys from the 1st Division.

"Put your hands up!" snapped a young lieutenant with a cocked pistol. "You're under arrest as German spies!"

Wolf tried vainly to identify Doug and himself. Their captor sneered, "How stupid do you think I am? No American general ever wore a sloppy cap like that, a non-regulation coat and—ye gods!—a woollen scarf. Besides, you dumb kraut, no American brass would ever be *this* far ahead of our lines!"

The "spies" were marched a mile as captives before a patrol from the Rainbow identified them and won their release. Doug turned to Wolf and chuckled, "How am I ever going to explain to my grandchildren that I was captured by the Americans?"

The war ended five days later, bringing to a close four years of world madness during which 65 million men had been mobilized into armies; 8 million had been killed; 22 million had been wounded; and 7,750,000 had been held in prison camps.

MacArthur came out of the holocaust almost a legendary figure, a "soldier's soldier" who had been wounded three times, decorated thirteen times, cited for extreme bravery in action seven times. Secretary of War Baker publicly hailed him as "our greatest front-line Commander." He was recommended a second time for the Congressional Medal of Honor, but once again his talent for making enemies in high places lost him the award. This time his name was struck from the list by General Pershing.

Doug spent five months in the Army of Occupation as head of the Rainbow. He told Wolf privately that he considered the military occupation a mistake. "It will only embitter the Germans further and make them determined to get revenge just as soon as they can raise another army."

When the Rainbow Division was finally ordered home in April 1919, they left behind three thousand of their dead in France. Over thirteen thousand Rainbow men had been wounded in battle; 205 had been awarded the Distinguished Service Cross; and only 102 had been taken prisoner. Doug MacArthur's faith in the Rainbow had been brilliantly vindicated. In the years that followed he was never too busy to see any man who had once worn the proud divisional patch.

Some of the Army's top brass was on hand to welcome the ship that brought the Fighting 42nd home. They were scandalized when the Commander of the Rainbow disembarked wearing a huge raccoon coat with a big woollen scarf wound around his neck.

A cloudy-faced major general, his brass fittings superbly polished, was heard to mutter in disgust to his home-front colleagues: "What *are* we going to do with that fellow?"

6
MacArthur Buys a New Hat

Doug was wearing his floppy, bedraggled cap when he reported to the office of General Peyton C. March, Army Chief of Staff, as ordered on a bright May morning in 1919. March, wincing at the cap, told him, "Mac, I've got a tough job for you. I want you to take over West Point as Superintendent."

A warm look of pleased surprise softened the angular severity of MacArthur's features. The honor was unprecedented. No officer as young as thirty-nine had ever commanded the Academy. But there were thorns on the rose. Forty years behind the times, West Point had degenerated during the war into an "officer factory," turning out "one-year wonders." There was practically nothing left of its curriculum, traditions, and honor system.

"One word of advice," March told MacArthur. "Will you for heaven's sake show up at the Point in a regulation Army hat? The diehards at the Academy are going to fight your changes hard enough without infuriating them further by that crazy cap!"

Doug jubilantly wired the news to his mother and brother. Mary MacArthur was living with Arthur's family at the naval base in San Diego. Arthur was married to an admiral's daughter, and was the father of five children. During the war he had fought with distinction as commander of a destroyer. Doug asked his mother to come to West Point and live there with him. It would be like coming home for her, too.

There was deep nostalgic pleasure in once more feeling the cool winds blowing from the Hudson, smelling the hallowed mustiness of the corridors in the old Academy buildings, hearing the sharp, birdlike cries of command from the drill field.

But MacArthur soon found that General March had not exaggerated the magnitude of the job he had on his hands. Morale was low, with a large number of cadet resignations; there were no disciplined standards of behavior; the instruction was hopelessly outdated and inadequate; officers on the faculty were balky about accepting changes.

"It's a mess, Mother!" Doug fumed, pacing the spacious living-room of the Superintendent's quarters. "I hardly recognize the Academy as the same place I was so proud to graduate from sixteen years ago. I've been handed a hopeless job!"

"Of course," Mary MacArthur agreed blandly. "What did you expect? Why else would they have picked the one officer they know can be depended on to do the impossible?"

He grinned, bent over, and kissed her cheek. "Mother, you always know just the right thing to say, don't you?"

Against faculty resistance MacArthur expanded and enriched the liberal arts courses, establishing new departments of History, Economics, and Government. He brought in top instructors to teach the latest developments in aerodynamics, chemistry, and electricity, and told them to pour it on the cadets, showing no mercy. He silenced faculty protests by asking, "How long are we going on preparing for the War of 1812?"

One professor, a colonel, was furious at Doug's proposal to institute a rigorous two-year course in English. At a board meeting he interrupted MacArthur to denounce the idiocy of wasting so much of a soldier's time teaching him how to handle words instead of weapons.

Doug endured the colonel's antediluvian prating as long as he could. Never a man to tolerate fools easily, he roared, "Sit down, sir—I have the floor! I think your own impoverished speech proves my case for the need of an officer to learn how to present his views in an intelligent and convincing manner. Without this ability an officer may have the finest judgment in the world, he may even be as wise as Solomon, yet his influence will be practically negligible. We are not training military weapons at West Point, sir—we are training military *minds!* Without a solid grounding in English, no officer can either grasp or communicate the subtleties and complexities of international conflicts in the twentieth century. The pen, sir, is *still* mightier than the sword!"

MacArthur's plans had to be approved by the Academic Board of West Point, which was dominated by older faculty members who regarded him as an upstart and outsider. Doug used every trick he knew to fight them and force them to accept his reforms. Once his adjutant asked whether a scheduled Board meeting should be called for 11:00 a.m.

"No," MacArthur replied swiftly. "Call the meeting for 4:30 p.m. I want the so-and-so's to come here hungry—I'll keep them here until I get what I want!" And he did.

One secret of his unique genius for command was apparent in his daily routine at the Academy. He never let himself get bogged down in petty details, but always made swift decisions on minor matters to allow himself ample leisure for serious thought.

"It's amazing," he once observed, "how many officers in high places survive by reflexes alone. Lots of them haven't had a single original thought in the last twenty years!"

He arrived at his office at 11:00 a.m. to give his staff time to get the morning's problems organized for him. In less than an hour he disposed of them all, along with his mail. The next hour he saw officers who had business with him. Then he went home for lunch with his mother, heeded her reminder to wear his overshoes or a muffler, and returned at 3:00 p.m. for official meetings until 4:30 or 5:00 p.m. All business moved smoothly with deceptive speed and calm, reflecting Doug's brilliant talent for swift appraisal and decision.

Once when he was home ill, he was phoned by his adjutant, Colonel Louis E. Hibbs, who asked if MacArthur wanted him to bring over the day's papers to be signed.

"Bring over the papers that are going to win or lose a war," Doug replied laconically. "You sign the others."

The change in military climate at West Point was unmistakable in less than six months. Greatly pleased, Secretary of War Baker made MacArthur a permanent brigadier general—the youngest in the Regular Army. This outraged many older officers who had also been temporary generals during the war, but now had been reduced to their old ranks of major or lieutenant colonel.

MacArthur's years as Superintendent at West Point were spent, for the most part, in lonely isolation. Only the companionship of his mother provided the spark of human warmth that kept him from becoming wholly austere and aloof.

"When you get to be a general, Louie," he once confided sadly in his adjutant, "you haven't any friends."

The man Doug felt closest to at West Point was Chaplain Clayton "Buck" Wheat, an intelligent, sports-minded man who shared MacArthur's conviction that athletics were next to godliness. One Sunday afternoon Wheat was depressed by the sight of cadets gloomily wandering around the post, and staring out barracks windows, because there was nothing else for them to do. On an impulse he called on Doug at home.

"General," he said, "why can't our boys use the plain on Sunday afternoon to practice baseball, tennis, or golf?"

The young Superintendent looked at him in surprise, and lit a favorite corncob pipe. "I never thought I'd hear a suggestion like that from a chaplain! You know, of course, that we'd be smothered in protests from religious groups?"

"We could take the edge off any complaints," Wheat pointed out eagerly, "if I played with the boys myself."

Doug's eyes glowed in approval. "Grand idea, Buck! Let's get the boys out under the blue sky. I'm with you all the way—and I think God would be on our side, too!"

There was a storm of outside protest, but MacArthur and the chaplain stood firm, with the enthusiastic support of the student body. Sunday afternoon at the Point became a happy occasion for competitive sports. But Doug didn't stop there. He made physical training and intramural sports compulsory, for officers and faculty as well as cadets. "Upon the fields of friendly strife," he wrote in an Academy memo, "are sown the seeds that upon other fields, in other days, will bear the fruits of victory."

An old star on West Point's baseball team, as well as a lifelong baseball fan, Doug naturally had a special affection for the Academy's nine. Despite his encouragement, Army lost to Navy ignominiously for two straight years. In May of 1921, however, the Army nine defeated Navy by 8 to 7, and a jubilant uproar swept through the Academy.

Point regulations forbade a "shirttail parade" after lights out, but promptly at midnight the whole cadet Corps gathered on the Plain, built a bonfire, and snake-danced past the Superintendent's quarters. The wildly noisy celebration lasted until dawn.

Promptly the next morning MacArthur rang for his commandant general, John Danford. Face solemn, he pinched his sharp nose and said, "Quite a racket last night, wasn't there?"

"Yes, sir," Danford replied apprehensively.

"How many cadets did you 'skin' for it, John?"

Danford sucked in his breath. "None, sir."

Doug jumped up and banged his fist on the desk. "Good!" he grinned. "I nearly got out of bed and joined them myself!"

Despite his understanding that "boys will be boys," MacArthur nevertheless insisted on stern discipline in important areas of behavior. He brought back the honor system to the Point, insisting that "West Point men have to be clean, live clean, and think clean." Cadets who did not keep their word were given short shrift.

When one cadet cheated, Doug immediately dismissed him from the Academy. Despite powerful pressure from the War Department in Washington on behalf of the boy's father, MacArthur refused reinstatement. "That young man committed an offense against the honor of the Corps," he told Washington firmly. "He shall never return to the Academy so long as I am its superintendent!"

In exchange for expecting West Pointers to act like gentlemen, Doug won their admiring cooperation by treating them like gentlemen. He granted weekend leave to cadets with good grades, and arranged for spending money so that cadets from poor families would not be socially embarrassed on leave with more affluent cadets. He allowed upper-classmen to smoke pipes and cigars in their rooms. Remembering too well his own bitter experience as a plebe, he abolished all hazing activities as degrading and sadistic.

Once a hazing did take place without the knowledge of the first captain, led by a superior cadet named George Olmstead. As soon as MacArthur heard about it, he promptly ordered Olmstead reduced to ranks. Asked why Olmstead should be punished for the incident, Doug's reply was illuminating: "If I had been first captain when something like this happened, I would have personally accepted full responsibility for any action the Corps took, even though I had no knowledge or part in it. That is the responsibility of leadership."

The following spring, noting that Olmstead had taken his demotion manfully, continuing to "soldier," MacArthur made him a cadet captain shortly before graduation.

Members of Doug's staff were also expected to assume full responsibility for anything that went wrong in their bailiwicks, whether they were to blame or not. One day after a fire at the Academy the Quartermaster came to see MacArthur.

"General," he panted unhappily, "the fire reached the firehouse, and the fire engine burned up. I think we'd better report that right away so we can get a replacement quickly."

Doug glared at him. "Sir, get your own fire engine if you have to build it yourself. I will not—repeat *not*—report a fire engine being burned in our firehouse!"

In 1922 MacArthur's enemies suddenly had their first chance to rub their hands in anticipation of change in their favor. Warren Harding succeeded Woodrow Wilson as President, and appointed a new Army Chief of Staff—General John J. Pershing. Army brass knew that Old Black Jack had no great love for Doug MacArthur, whom he considered an impertinent if obviously brilliant upstart.

Another old wartime acquaintance turned up unexpectedly one night as Doug was being driven back to the Point from an evening spent in New York. A man with a flashlight flagged the car to a stop, then suddenly drew a pistol.

"Hand over your money!" he rasped at MacArthur.

The tall military figure in the back seat crossed his legs calmly. "I've got about forty dollars in my pocket, but you'll have to whip me to get it. Put up your gun, and I'll come out and fight you fair and square for it."

The thug angrily flicked the safety off his gun and waved it menacingly. "Don't get cute with me! Hand that money over or I'll blow your head off!" He trained the flashlight beam squarely on Doug's face, then suddenly gasped. "Holy smokes! Ain't you—General MacArthur of the Rainbow?"

Doug nodded curtly. A look of embarrassment crossed the hold-up man's features. "I was a sergeant in Wild Bill Donovan's outfit, sir. I—well, it's been tough since the war, and I've got two kids. . . ." He put the gun in his pocket sheepishly. "I'm sorry, General. Tell your driver to go on."

MacArthur put his hand in his pocket, took out a purse, and held all the bills out of the car window. "I want to buy your gun, sergeant," he said crisply.

The amazed veteran surrendered the gun and accepted the money. Doug examined the weapon briefly, then holding it by the barrel, flung it out the opposite window into the Hudson.

"Drive on," he ordered his chauffeur. When he reached the Point he made no effort to notify the State Police.

Doug's loneliness suddenly came to an abrupt end in 1922 when he met and danced with a pretty socialite named Louise Brooks at Tuxedo, the society resort west of the Point. She was a gay and charming divorcee with two children, and had been the toast of the American colony in Paris since the war. Doug fell in love with her almost instantly, and she was equally smitten with the most famous bachelor catch of the day. He began a whirlwind courtship, undaunted even by the unsettling discovery that Louise was the official Washington hostess for none other than General Pershing, who was also her suitor.

More worrisome to Doug was the disapproval of his mother. Mary MacArthur's keen intuition told her that a sophisticated woman like Louise Brooks, who loved parties and the wealthy society in which she had been reared, would not fit well into military life—the life to which her son had dedicated himself. Besides, it is questionable whether Mrs. MacArthur would have found *any* woman worthy of her brilliant son, after forty-two years of being the only important woman in his life.

MacArthur's marriage to Louise Brooks, in a fashionable ceremony at Palm Beach, Florida, on February 14, 1922, was deeply upsetting to his mother. She signified her disapproval by refusing to attend. Shortly afterward she became chronically ill.

Another ominous note was struck on the wedding day. With the ceremony scheduled for 4:00 p.m., Doug found Louise on a stepladder decorating the villa where they were being married long after she should have been dressed in her bridal gown.

"Really, Louise," he reproached her in shocked tones, "there is such a thing as preparedness, you know."

She came down from the stepladder, her beautiful eyes alive with fire. "I am not accustomed to being lectured, Douglas," she said coldly. "Certainly not by my fiance!"

It was not an auspicious beginning. Nor did the newspapers help much by such headlines as: MARRIAGE OF MARS AND MILLIONS.

Each one of the 1,700 cadets at West Point received a small white monogrammed box tied with red, white, and blue ribbon, containing a piece of wedding cake. When MacArthur brought his bride back to the Academy, the cadets were invited to call and meet the Superintendent's new wife in groups of fifty.

But they were not to know her for long. As a rule the post of Superintendent of West Point was a four-year detail. Doug had held the job for only a little under three years at the time of his marriage when, less than two months after he had snatched Louise Brooks out of General Pershing's orbit, Black Jack "relieved" him of the West Post command and ordered him overseas to Manila.

Washington buzzed with one-word gossip: "Exile!" Reporters pounced on Pershing and demanded to know whether Doug was being banished because of his marriage. "Poppycock!" snorted Black Jack. "It's all idle gossip without the slightest foundation!"

If Doug also thought that his transfer to a foreign post was more than a curious coincidence, he said nothing. Besides, he had not seen the Philippines in twenty years, and that exotic land still exercised a magical attraction for him. He hoped that Louise would find island life as fascinating as he had.

But even before their ship sailed, she felt desperately homesick for the gay society life she was leaving behind.

7

Peacetime Villain

From the moment they moved into a large old Manila residence with beautiful gardens and a view of the whole city, Louise was unhappy. She hated the dullness of routine army life, as predictable as the afternoon heat that blazed like a furnace. Life in Manila was a far cry from what she had been accustomed to in Paris, Washington, New York, and Palm Beach. Resenting her husband's constant absorption in military matters, Louise began to urge him to resign from the Army and return to the States.

Doug was shocked at the suggestion. "The Army is my whole life, Louise," he tried to make her understand.

"But it's not mine!" she cried. "I hate it here!"

He tried appealing to her patriotism. "Someday the Japanese are going to attack the Philippines. We'll have to fight it out on the Bataan Peninsula. That's why I'm working so hard on a complete survey and defense plan of Bataan. I couldn't leave now, dear. What I'm doing is too important."

"Oh, and *I'm* not? You've even got more time for your precious Filipino friends than you do for me!"

This was another sore point between them. Louise preferred the company of the white American social set in Manila, but Doug's dinner guests were primarily Filipinos. He had built a close friendship with Manuel Quezon, President of the Philippine Senate, who was destined to be the country's first President after independence.

In this MacArthur was motivated by the desire to protect his country's interests in the Far Pacific. He knew that white colonialism was finished in Asia, and that if the threat of Japan's modern imperialism were to be beaten off, America would need real friends in the Philippines. Doug fought a one-man crusade against the prejudice and snobbery of the American upper crust in Manila. By going out of his way to show publicly that he accepted Filipinos as social equals, he hoped to set an example for Army and government officials.

Instead, he was despised by them—as an upstart radical out to overthrow the barriers of class and racial superiority which they had modeled after the British colonial system. But MacArthur won the respect and affection of the people who counted—the Filipinos.

So there was friction between him and Louise, and it was very much a question who would capitulate. Both were stubborn and strong-willed and only an act of fate saved them from the need to compromise.

The cable from Doug's sister-in-law, Mary McCulla MacArthur, read: MOTHER CRITICALLY ILL. COME HOME AT ONCE.

On February 11, 1923, MacArthur sailed from Manila accompanied by Louise and her two children, who had been ill with malaria. Although the occasion was a gloomy one, Louise was not sorry to have the opportunity of escaping home. For Doug the long trip back to Washington, where his mother was now living with Arthur's family, was filled with anxiety. Would he be too late? But his mother brightened and began to recover almost from the moment she saw her younger son.

"You're the tonic she needed," Arthur told him a little ruefully. "Let's face it, Doug—you always were!"

His mother recovered rapidly and Doug and Louise, much against her will, returned to Manila. Then in December he received word of Arthur's sudden death at forty-seven, of appendicitis. Doug swallowed hard to choke back the emotion that shook him. He remembered as though it were yesterday the scenes of his boyhood—lying on the floor with his brother at army posts, listening to Father reading aloud to them from the lives of American heroes; riding and hunting with Arthur across the desert plains; learning together with Mother in the quarters they shared at each new army post.

He felt terribly alone.

Early in 1925 his tour of duty in the Philippines was over. He returned home with a War Department promotion to the rank of major general, and command of the 3rd Corps in Baltimore. Louise was delighted. At her insistence they moved into her country estate at Rainbow Hill, Maryland. Now Louise had her way, and they were caught up in the social whirl she loved.

After one party jammed with the kind of Washington parasites Doug despised, he returned home in an ugly temper.

"Louise," he said tightly as they prepared for bed, "I heard something tonight that made me mad. There's gossip all over Washington that *you* were responsible for my promotion. With a private letter to Pershing."

"Oh?" Louise raised her eyebrows. "It's a silly rumor. But even if it were true, what would be so awful about a wife helping her husband's career?"

Doug looked at her helplessly. "If you don't know, I don't think I could tell you!" He added sternly, "Just remember one thing—any promotion I don't earn I will not accept!"

She turned away without replying.

In October 1925 MacArthur was appointed to sit on the court-martial board trying Brigadier General William "Billy" Mitchell for publicly criticizing the military's failure to develop America's air power, and demanding a separate Air Force. Found guilty, Mitchell promptly resigned to continue his fight as a civilian. Reporters besieged Doug, whom they knew to have been a friend of Mitchell's, to tell them how he had voted, but he maintained a stony silence.

Those who disliked MacArthur lost no time in branding him a Pontius Pilate who had martyred his friend, and who was opposed to the idea of an independent Air Corps. This made Doug a villain in the eyes of flying crews up to and through World War II. But he never once revealed the truth—that his had been the only voice on the court-martial board to agree with Billy Mitchell on the need for a separate military command for air power, and to fight for Mitchell's right to speak out to the nation.

Mitchell himself told General George C. Kenney years later, "Doug MacArthur is a grand guy and a true friend. I'm very fond of him. Some day people will realize how good a friend of mine he was back there in 1925."

As commander of the 3rd Corps in Baltimore, Doug introduced the same strenuous athletic program for troops that he had brought to West Point. This led to his selection in 1928 as president of the American Olympic Committee and director of the Olympic team which he took to Holland. He had one succinct bit of advice for his athletes: "Good sportsmanship at all times, gentlemen . . . but keep in mind that we did not come here to lose gracefully!"

In September Doug was ordered to return to Manila in command of the Department of the Philippines. Louise refused to go back with him. They parted sadly, but without hard feelings, and their marriage was dissolved in June 1927.

Putting aside personal sorrows, Doug flung himself into the tasks of preparing his Filipino friends for independence, and for the defense of the islands against the Japanese invasion that he knew was on Tokyo's timetable of conquest.

Shortly after taking command of the Department of the Philippines, his adjutant general presented him with a huge bound volume of rulings issued by all the Department commanders who had preceded Doug. "These will give you the precedents for solving any problem that may arise, sir," he said.

"Burn them," Doug replied promptly. "When any problem comes up, I'll make the decision immediately—on the merits of the case, not on outworn precedents!"

By 1930 General Pershing had retired as Chief of Staff, and Secretary of War Patrick Hurley wanted to give the job to Douglas MacArthur. Pershing was vehemently opposed, but President Herbert Hoover approved. So at age fifty MacArthur was summoned home to become one of the youngest Chiefs of Staff in American history, having achieved the pinnacle his father had failed to reach. The first person he permitted to see the shiny new four stars on his shoulder was his mother. Mary MacArthur, now seventy-eight, embraced him with moist-eyed pride.

"If only your father could have lived to see you now," she whispered. "Douglas, you're everything he wanted to be!"

He took her to live with him in the Chief of Staff's quarters at Fort Myer outside Washington. There was widespread bitterness at his elevation to the heights of rank and position at so young an age, when much older officers of great experience were still majors and colonels.

The criticism grew steadily louder when MacArthur failed to convince a tough, economy-minded Congress to appropriate enough money for military defense. These were depression days, and there was a strong isolationist movement which believed in ignoring the storm clouds boiling overseas.

"An adequate army is to the nation what an adequate fire department is to the city," MacArthur pleaded with Congress. "The Japanese are marching in Asia, and Hitler's Nazi followers in Europe are preparing for world conquest. We must be prepared! We have only 12,000 officers and 125,000 men to defend America—and less than half of them are service troops!"

Deeply worried, MacArthur decided to tour Europe in 1931–32 to study at firsthand the military situation there. While he was abroad, Hoover cabled him to attend the Disarmament Conference at the League of Nations in Geneva. Doug flatly refused.

"The way to end war is to outlaw war," he cabled Hoover, "not to disarm!" The press began to pillory him as a warmonger who was itching to drag America into another war to play hero again.

Upon his return MacArthur ignored these attacks, but added fuel to the flames by fighting and pleading with Congress to restore slashes in the Regular Army budget. Almost single-handed, he fought for two months to defeat a bill to drop two thousand officers from the Army, and finally prevailed. He won by proving that although we were the wealthiest of the six world powers in 1932, we had the tiniest army per capita of them all.

Many Congressmen were openly hostile to MacArthur, not only for his military views, but because of his austere manner and too-tailored appearance. Just before one hearing in the House of Representatives, a Congressman sighed to his colleague, "Well, it's about time to go over and hear what the Dude has to say."

At the hearing one Congressman lost his temper and called MacArthur a "thief of the public budget." Another sneered at him as a "polished popinjay," and a third called him a "bellicose swashbuckler." Doug listened to these jibes with pale cheeks and flashing eyes. Finally he could endure no more and stood up.

"Gentlemen," he said in a voice of steel, "you have insulted me. But I in my profession am as high as you in your profession. When you are ready to apologize, I shall return."

He walked out of the hearing room. In a little while he received a Committee apology, and returned to fight for the stronger America he believed in. Perhaps at no time in Doug MacArthur's career did he ever have to humble his pride as much as during his battles with Congress.

"I have humiliated myself seeking allotments to replace leaking, slumlike barracks housing our soldiers," he admitted to friends. "I have almost licked the boots of certain gentlemen to get funds for motorization and mechanization of the Army. Unless we move quickly we will be a beaten nation, paying huge indemnities after the next war."

Against almost insuperable odds, MacArthur fought for and won America's first real tank corps, the beginnings of an air arm, the semi-automatic Garand rifle for infantry, a plan for wartime mobilization of industry, and a Selective Service plan.

"Tanks, planes, submarines will be the decisive weapons in the next war," Doug insisted. "Mass movements of airplanes and huge concentrations of tanks will win the battles."

His greatest help was the support of Secretary of War Hurley, who trusted MacArthur's military foresight. "Thank God the General is right most of the time," Hurley sighed. "It's almost impossible to convince him when he's wrong. Takes all night and all the next day and sometimes a month or two!"

Perhaps the worst blow to MacArthur's public image was the affair of the Bonus Army, which involved what Doug called "the most distasteful duty of my whole career." At the height of the depression fifteen million Americans were without jobs, and 20,000 unemployed veterans came to Washington with their wives and children, to pressure Congress into voting immediately for a two billion dollar cash bonus to all World War I veterans.

For two months the Bonus Army camped in lean-tos, shanties, and tents on Anacostia Flats and elsewhere, announcing they would stay there until Congress paid them off. They had one sympathizer in high places—Doug MacArthur. Many of the Bonus Army were his own men who had served under him in France. He set up rolling Army kitchens to feed them, but was ordered to discontinue this humane practice.

On July 28, 1932 rioting caused President Hoover to order Secretary Hurley to drive the Bonus Army squatters out of their encampments, and out of Washington. Hurley passed the order on to MacArthur, warning, "It's a dirty job, Doug. Better turn it over to your aide—what's his name?—Major Dwight Eisenhower."

MacArthur shook his head. "It could be the kiss of death for any junior officer's career. If the job has to be done, I consider it my responsibility to do it myself."

He hoped that his wartime prestige would persuade the veterans to disperse peacefully, and to show himself one of them he put on his World War I uniform with eight rows of ribbons. To make sure he was seen, he mounted a white horse at the head of tanks and cavalry commanded by Major George S. Patton. Doug had warned him to use only tear gas, if necessary.

As the troops marched down Pennsylvania Avenue, the Bonus Marchers booed and threw bricks. Tear-gas shells were lobbed back, and MacArthur himself received a lungful. There was a wild stampede among a mob of ten thousand spectators who had gathered to watch the spectacle, and many were injured. At bayonet point the troops reached and burned down the shacktowns set up by the veterans, but not before MacArthur fed the dispossessed men and their families, and provided many with gas and oil for their cars to get them back home.

The next morning Doug woke up to find himself crucified in the press as "a bemedalled Prussian bully," "the Number One brass hat," "the brutal enemy of the enlisted men." Along with Hoover he was charged with "murdering veterans on the streets of Washington." He sighed and kept silent, reflecting that a soldier's job is often hardest in peacetime.

The Bonus Army affair helped sweep Hoover out of the White House in 1932, replacing him with an old friend of Doug's. Although Franklin Delano Roosevelt and MacArthur liked and respected each other, each held strong opinions about the needs of America which often clashed violently.

Their first fight was not long in coming. Doug was appalled when he heard that Roosevelt wanted more cuts in the Army's budget to lower government spending, in order to expand new social services to get the country out of the depression.

"Mr. President," MacArthur appealed, "with the Japanese marching through Manchuria and China, and Hitler and Mussolini building war machines in Europe, is this a time to weaken America's defenses? Your budget would force me to put our troops on half rations, and to suspend target practice because we won't have enough money for ammunition!"

Roosevelt's eyes flashed. Like MacArthur, he was a man of flamboyant egotism, and did not take kindly to being told what to do. "It's my job as President to run the affairs of the country," he rebuked Doug sharply, "and I will brook no interference!"

"If you pursue this policy, Mr. President, you will destroy the American Army. I have no choice but to oppose you publicly. I shall ask for my immediate relief as Chief of Staff, and for retirement from the Army. Then I shall take this fight directly to the people!"

Saluting, he turned on his heel and left the White House sick with anguish. Now his neck was on the chopping block, and he had placed it there himself. But he felt that if his life as a soldier had any meaning at all, that meaning could only have validity in the courage of his convictions.

Fortunately Roosevelt was too intelligent to let pride get the better of his judgment. Thinking over MacArthur's arguments, he came to the conclusion that his unyielding Chief of Staff was probably right. Besides, if serious trouble did lie ahead, the United States could not afford to lose Douglas MacArthur as the head of its armed forces. Roosevelt quietly spread the word to drop the fight for slicing the military budget.

Far from holding a grudge, Roosevelt frequently invited MacArthur to the White House to discuss New Deal problems. Doug was puzzled. One day he ventured to ask, "Mr. President, why do you ask a military man to give you opinions about civilian matters?"

Roosevelt's smile adapted itself to the cigarette holder perennially jutting from between his teeth. "Douglas, to me you are a symbol of the conscience of America."

MacArthur was convinced that it was only a matter of time before Japan would fling itself at America's throat, and that the Philippines would be struck first. "The Philippines must be defended at all costs," he warned Congress. "The United States must build the strongest defenses on all our islands in the Pacific—Wake, Guam, Hawaii, and the Philippines. There is no time to be lost!"

Congress responded in March 1934, by passing the Tydings-McDuffie Act, guaranteeing the Philippines full independence in 1946, and pledging her defense by America until that time. But Congressional committees continued to carve slices out of the military budget. A bill was even introduced to deny General of the Armies John J. Pershing a pension of $18,000 a year.

Doug had small reason to love crusty old Black Jack, but the ingratitude of this move against Pershing was too much for his sense of justice. He appeared before the Senate Appropriations Committee to fight and defeat the bill. Pershing, then seventy-two, wrote MacArthur a personal letter of thanks.

Doug's four-year term as Chief of Staff was supposed to end in November 1934, but Roosevelt insisted that he stay on. This was the first time in American history that a Chief of Staff succeeded himself. "I must always find a way to keep Douglas close to me," Roosevelt confided in his aide Louis Howe. "If we ever have another A.E.F., he's the man to take over."

But MacArthur's refusal to bend his principles to expediency brought America's two strong leaders into continual collision course. In March 1935, Roosevelt wanted Congress to give him personal power to increase or reduce the size of the Army, a control which had always been exercised by Congress. Doug appeared on Capitol Hill to protest this usurpation of power by the Executive Branch.

"The President, splendid soldier as he is, and understanding the problems of National defense as he does, cannot be expected to make decisions which have not only involved the professional thought of the Army for years, but have engaged the attention of the Congressional Committees for weeks and months at a time." Roosevelt's bill was voted down.

Advisers around FDR inflamed his anger at this act of "outrageous disloyalty and insubordination." MacArthur could no longer be tolerated in high office—he obviously had no intention of playing on the team. The opportunity to get rid of him gracefully came abruptly in a summer visitor to the White House. Manuel Quezon was soon to be inaugurated as first President of the Philippine Commonwealth, a new caretaker government which would rule until Independence Day.

Roosevelt hinted that Doug might be available to return to Manila with Quezon, to help establish Philippine defenses. Quezon lost no time in begging for MacArthur as his military adviser. FDR agreed "reluctantly," and also offered Doug the post of first US High Commissioner to the Philippines. MacArthur coolly refused, preferring a completely free hand in Manila.

He resigned as Chief of Staff and accepted Quezon's offer with only one stipulation—that his eighty-three-year-old mother accompany him to his new post. When mother and son left Washington, MacArthur's jubilant enemies congratulated themselves that they had once more succeeded in sending him into exile.

But Doug was less angry than grieved. "It's probably a good thing that I am going to the Philippines now," he told his mother as their ship sailed. "The job that must be done there is urgent. But I hate to leave the country in the hands of the politicians who have banished me."

"They have not banished you, Douglas," his mother told him, proudly lifting her wrinkled face to his. "*You* have banished *them*. The real spirit of America will always be wherever Douglas MacArthur is!"

8
Years of Exile

MacArthur's years in the nation's capital had unquestionably embittered him. He took with a grain of salt Roosevelt's final words to him on the eve of his departure: "Doug, if war comes, don't wait for orders to return here. Grab the first transportation you can find. I want you to command my armies." MacArthur was wryly aware that if his star had not already set in Washington, it would soon sink out of sight with his absence.

When he sailed for the Philippines with his mother on the *President Hoover,* he took with him a small staff of picked men including forty-five-year-old Major Eisenhower as his Chief of Staff, and Major James Ord as Eisenhower's deputy. Arthur's widow, Mary McCulla MacArthur, had agreed to come along to look after her ailing mother-in-law. Each day of the voyage Doug spent hours at his mother's bedside, discussing his plans for Philippine defense.

Mary observed the closeness of her brother-in-law and his mother with admiration tinged by worry. "Doug," she said softly one day, "Mother's desperately sick."

He nodded wanly. "I'd hoped that the sea voyage would do her some good. But Manila will help. All the sunshine. . ."

"The best medicine is her talks with you. She lives for them, Doug. Don't get too busy for them in Manila, will you?"

"Never, Mary," he promised solemnly.

As the *President Hoover* plunged westward, MacArthur roughed out a design for the defense of the Philippines against the attack by Japan he anticipated. It would take $80 million and ten years, becoming complete in 1946, when the US had promised the Philippines independence. His plans called for conscripting and training forty thousand men a year; building a ten-division reserve militia of four hundred thousand; developing a fleet of fast PT boats; and an air force to guard the Islands' coast and skies.

Between working out details with Eisenhower and Ord, and visiting with his mother, MacArthur had little time for shipboard relaxation. But his mother was insistent that he meet a young woman on board named Jean Marie Faircloth. Doug knew that his mother had been looking for another wife for him since 1929.

"Really, Mother, I'm much too busy—"

"She's a perfectly lovely girl, Douglas," his mother persisted. "Pretty, with a lovely smile and a charming personality. She's from Murfreesboro, Tennessee. Her grandfather was at Missionary Ridge with your father. On the opposite side, of course! Her whole family is Army, and she loves the traditions. She's just cut out to be a soldier's wife—"

"All right, Mother," Doug surrendered with a mock groan. "Introduce me. But wait a day before you post the banns!"

To MacArthur's surprise, Jean Faircloth turned out to be even more fascinating than his mother had claimed. She was a tiny, hundred-pound brunette of thirty-five, sparkling and vivacious, yet so comfortable to be with that he felt remarkably relaxed and happy in her company. Ignoring the twenty-year difference in their ages, he began to court her assiduously. When the ship stopped at Honolulu, he had Jean's stateroom filled with roses, along with a card that read: "Love, from Douglas."

When Mrs. MacArthur learned that Jean planned to leave the ship to stay with British friends in Hong Kong, she persuaded her to continue on instead to Manila to attend the colorful ceremonies marking the inauguration of Manuel Quezon as first President of the Philippines Commonwealth.

Soon after the MacArthurs took up residence in the Manila Hotel, Mother MacArthur's illness grew worse. The doctor attending her told Doug that he needed a special serum to save her, but there was none in the islands. Desperate, MacArthur sent off a frantic radio appeal to Washington. A Clipper plane was dispatched with the serum from California.

Meanwhile Mary MacArthur was sinking fast. When Jean Faircloth visited her bedside, the dying woman gripped her hand and whispered, "Don't leave Douglas. He is going to love you very much." Before the serum could arrive, she lapsed into a coma and died in the arms of the son she had reared to greatness.

Her loss shook Doug more profoundly than any deprivation he had ever suffered in his life. He could not really believe that she was finally gone, that the beautiful relationship they had shared for so many years was over. It was MacArthur's sister-in-law who put into words the feelings in his heart that were too emotion-charged for him to express.

"Mother MacArthur," she told reporters, "was a wonderful woman and a most devoted and loving mother to her two sons as well as to me. She was the most generous and just person I have ever known and *a real soldier.*"

For a few weeks Doug was almost a silent recluse, inconsolable. But as he recovered from the shock of his loss, he turned increasingly to Jean Faircloth for the intimacy he missed. Gradually the demands of his bold plan for defense of the Philippines forced him to turn his mind back to military thoughts.

The plan delighted Quezon, who insisted that MacArthur accept a gold baton and the rank of Grand Field Marshal of the Philippines. The honor was somewhat ironic, since it would make him Grand Field Marshal of a practically non-existent army. At a dinner given in his honor, when Doug was saluted by two Filipinos in uniform with ancient muskets, he grinned. "I didn't know I had two soldiers to start with."

He told Quezon he didn't think he ought to accept the grandiose title: "It might not be properly understood in my own country. They'll ask what right I have to accept a rank higher than my own country has to offer. I'll be accused of trying to become a 'Napoleon of the Islands.'"

"You should be accustomed to the sniping of jealous enemies by this time, Douglas," Quezon replied. "Besides, you will hurt the pride of my people if you refuse. With the gold baton in your hands, it will be easier to arouse their enthusiasm and support for the military program we must have."

As Jean Faircloth looked on proudly, Doug accepted the gold baton from Quezon's hands at a public ceremony. "This is a call of duty," he said sternly. "I cannot fail. By 1946 I will make of the Islands a Pacific Switzerland that would cost any invader five hundred thousand men, three years, and more than $5 billion to conquer!" He announced the establishment of a fine military academy to operate on the model of West Point, to give the Philippines a first-rate officers corps.

US civilian officials in Manila were dismayed, not only at MacArthur's grandiloquent title, but also by his $30,000 a year salary and the six-room, air-conditioned penthouse apartment he was given atop the new Manila Hotel. They attacked him privately for the "greed" which had brought him back to Manila to "set up a military dictatorship for Quezon."

Doug was stung by this backbiting and exploded. "I would not sell my sword!" But then he lapsed into tight-lipped silence, too proud and too busy to defend himself any further. He doggedly continued to work at building Philippine defenses, ignoring the backwash of criticism from Washington, as well as High Commissioner Frank Murphy's protest to the President that the Islands were not big enough for both MacArthur and himself.

Doug had his hands full trying to breathe life into his blueprint for military preparedness. The new Filipino legislature balked at voting the money he needed. The Moros, fierce Moslem tribesmen who had always fought national authority, refused to register for army duty. Other recruits were too illiterate and sickly to train properly. Much of the war materiel lent MacArthur by the American Army was hopelessly outmoded or rusty. No planes arrived, and reports from Washington hinted that his demand for PT boats was considered absurd by the Navy.

High Commissioner Murphy was relieved, and upon his return to the States wired Quezon that FDR wanted to see him at the White House during February 1937. Quezon asked Doug to go along to persuade Roosevelt to give them more military help. When they reached New York, MacArthur was stunned to learn that the White House knew nothing of the request forwarded by Murphy, and Murphy himself was away somewhere on vacation.

Doug went to the White House and asked the President's secretary, Ross McIntyre, for an appointment with FDR McIntyre coldly refused, stating that the President had not sent for Quezon and was under no obligation to receive him. Stunned, unable to understand such shocking hostility toward the Chief Executive of the Philippines, MacArthur insisted upon paying his personal respects to FDR He was reluctantly given a five-minute appointment. Doug took two hours. In no mood for tact or diplomacy, he angrily told Roosevelt it would be a blunder of the worst magnitude if Quezon were officially snubbed.

"Sir," he warned darkly, "the Filipinos would take it as proof that the United States has only disinterest and contempt for their country. This is exactly what Japan is telling them. If we have to go to war with the Japs, would you want to count on the help and loyalty of a country whose President you have rebuffed publicly in such a way as to humiliate him throughout Asia?"

Roosevelt's motives in this peculiar affair remained obscure, but Doug suspected that some of his advisers who disliked the Quezon–MacArthur team wanted the President to use this occasion to "cut them down to size." The mystery of the invitation extended by Murphy was never solved. In any event, Roosevelt was finally persuaded to relent and arranged an official tea party for the Filipino Chief Executive at the Hotel Mayflower.

During his talk with the President, MacArthur also tried to warn FDR about the folly of letting certain American groups continue to ship scrap iron, oil, and gas to Japan. "Mr. President," he pointed out, "the greed of these profiteers is placing the Philippines in peril. The Japs are hoarding these raw materials to use in a war against us. What is the point of my trying to build up the defenses of the Islands, if these profiteers are to be allowed to help the Japs tear them down?"

Roosevelt promised to give more thought to an embargo on oil and scrap iron shipments to Japan.

Doug had some personal business to attend to before he returned to Manila. Taking his leave of Quezon in Washington, he left for New York to meet Jean Faircloth, who had followed him to the States by plane. They were married quietly on April 30, 1937, in New York City's Municipal Building, with Doug wearing a simple brown civilian suit. *"This* job," he told reporters, "is going to last a long time."

They flew back to Manila the next day.

With Jean beside him, Doug looked and acted twenty years younger. She was an ideal soldier's wife—his mother had been right. Jean loved the Army, understood its necessities, enjoyed its traditions. Her warm, natural, unassuming manner quickly won over army wives of all ranks. MacArthur's associates noticed that he was beginning to lose some of his famous austerity as his personality mellowed under Jean's radiant love.

With quaint military gallantry, he addressed her gravely as "ma'am." Jean called him "the General," or when she was feeling mischievous, "Sir Boss." Once she teasingly asked him when he had first been sure that he loved her. Doug thought for a moment, then replied dryly, "When I found out that you were as fond of cowboy movies as I was. I knew then I'd never find another woman like you in a million years!"

Like his father before him, MacArthur spent almost every night in his personal library of almost eight thousand books, studying the plans and methods of the world's greatest military strategists. Jean not only understood, but every Christmas presented him with a biography of a Civil War general to add to his library.

Toward the end of 1937 Doug suddenly received orders to return to the United States. Shocked at this abrupt command to abandon his efforts to create a Philippine army, he suspected that there were forces close to the President which did not want to see the Islands become capable of self-defense. If Quezon had to rely on American military protection, independence for the Philippines could be postponed indefinitely.

Manuel Quezon was indignant to the point of tears. "But they cannot take you away from us, Douglas!" he exclaimed. "If we lose you now, the whole program will fall to pieces!"

Deeply troubled, Doug talked the dilemma over with Jean. "My duty to my country, as well as my duty to the Philippines, tells me that I ought to stay here and finish the job I came to do," he told her, his granite-like face shadowed with brooding. "I can't see any way out except to retire from the Army so that I can remain here as Quezon's military adviser."

"You will never do the wrong thing, dear," she reassured him warmly, "as long as you follow your conscience."

MacArthur submitted his resignation to the President. The news delighted his military enemies in Washington. Having helped to exile him in the Philippines, they were now highly satisfied to have him isolated there ten thousand miles from the sources of American military power and policy-making. Roosevelt accepted Doug's resignation with a graceful tribute: "Your record in war and in peace is a brilliant chapter of American history."

"Sounds like an obituary," Doug told Jean wryly. Then with some of his old arrogance he added, "They'd better not close the file on MacArthur yet. I've still got an important contribution to make here to the defense of America in the Pacific!"

On February 20th, 1938, when Doug was fifty-eight—still proudly erect, clear-eyed, and vigorous—Jean wrote a letter to her family in Tennessee. "I am praying," she told them, "it is a boy—to carry on the MacArthur military tradition."

The next day she presented Doug MacArthur with a son and heir, whom Doug promptly named Arthur in honor of his father, and in memory of his dead brother. Soon nicknamed "Sergeant," little Arthur opened up doors in his father s heart that no one had ever suspected were there. Visiting aides often found Grand Field Marshal MacArthur being ridden around the room by his little son, or singing duets with him while shaving.

But gloomier events were beginning to cast their shadows before them. In September 1939, Hitler's armies invaded Poland, touching off World War II. When England and France were suddenly plunged into war, the Congress that had sneered at Doug MacArthur's pleas for a stronger program of national defense now began frantically rushing through belated bills to speed up military production.

MacArthur's pleas that some of these new armaments be sent to the Philippines again fell on deaf ears. American strategy called for earmarking all excess armaments for England and France, to help them stop Hitler. The threat of Japan was shrugged off, even though the Nipponese had invaded Indo-China, and had signed a military alliance with Germany and Italy.

So bitter was Doug about Roosevelt's refusal to understand the equally grave threat in the Pacific that he wrote to an Army friend in the US, "I think the greatest disaster that could possibly visit the world would be Roosevelt's re-election as President of the United States." Having retired from the US Army, he was now free to speak his mind bluntly about the Commander-in-Chief of that Army.

But he was equally thwarted by the Philippine legislature, which cut the military budget sharply, and authorized the training of only half the men his plan called for. In addition, they refused to do anything about the Moras' refusal to register for the draft.

"No small nation or great one," MacArthur warned them angrily, "which is not willing to fight to the death for its freedom, is fit to enjoy it long!"

He worked long hours in his study, planning how best to mobilize his limited resources in a defense of the Islands if the Japs should strike without warning. A guest on the floor below, after enduring Doug's pacing back and forth overhead until 2:00 and 3:00 a.m., night after night, phoned the desk clerk to complain bitterly, "Doesn't that guy in the penthouse know what time it is?"

In April 1941, watching his country get ready for the war which he was now convinced was inevitable, Doug could no longer bear the thought that he was not in the uniform which he had devoted a whole lifetime to wearing. He wrote a surprisingly humble letter to Steve Early, FDR's press secretary and private adviser, asking Early to discuss with the President the possibility of recalling him to active service.

At first there was no reply, and Doug was plunged into gloom. "I guess I'm through," he sighed to Jean.

"Be patient, dear," she urged. "They're not exactly fools in Washington. Like you or not, they know they need you."

On July 26, 1941, less than five months before Pearl Harbor, Roosevelt recalled MacArthur to active service as a major general, and ordered him to take command of all American forces in the Far East, with the Philippine army as part of the American command. The following day Doug was promoted to the rank of lieutenant general.

Deeply moved at being able once more to put on his beloved uniform, MacArthur told Manila reporters in a choked voice, "America has ordered me to defend the Philippines. I must not fail America." Less solemnly he chuckled to Jean, "I feel like an old dog in a new uniform!"

But the new sixty-one-year-old Commander of USAFFE had only token forces for a Herculean job. Under him now were a mere nineteen thousand American and twenty thousand Filipino troops; eight thousand American and 150 Filipino air force personnel; about 250 planes; and a squadron or two of torpedo boats. Washington's rule-of-thumb was to send one plane to MacArthur for every fifty sent to Europe.

To make the most of his meager defenses, Doug carefully surveyed anew the battlegrounds he would choose when the Japs invaded. One of his aides remarked, "He sensed where the enemy would strike, and he made certain that he knew every rock, every tree, every creek, every path, every bridge." MacArthur was convinced that there were only two beaches in the Manila archipelago where the Japs could land; and that he could drive them back into the sea. In this he seriously underestimated the Japanese, but so did the whole US War Department.

Doug's intimate knowledge of Japanese politics gave him a shrewder idea of what the Japs were up to than any of the top brass in Washington. On October 16, 1941 Japan's anti-American War Minister Hideki Tojo became Premier, and a month later sent two special envoys to Washington ostensibly to ease cold war tensions between the two nations. One of the envoys was a Tokyo diplomat named Kurusu.

"Something's fishy," MacArthur told his staff. "Kurusu is washed up in Japanese politics. Why would they send a man like that on an important peace mission? Unless he's simply being used as window dressing for something going on behind the scenes!"

Toward the end of November, General George C. Marshall, who was now Army Chief of Staff, notified Doug that he was convinced that war with Japan was inevitable, but he did not believe they would attack before April 1942. He advised MacArthur to be guided by this prognostication in making defense plans.

Side by side with this message on Doug's desk was a report from Manila's single radar set that Japanese reconnaissance planes had been tracked flying across Luzon. By the first week in December, Navy Intelligence men on Corregidor had cracked the secret Japanese codes. MacArthur was shown intercepted radio messages sent from Tokyo to the Japanese Embassy in Washington that left no doubt in his mind that a sneak attack was being mounted. But where?

When Doug went to bed Sunday night, December 8th, Manila time—which was still Saturday night in Hawaii—he was thinking of the twelve thousand miles of Philippine coastline it was his responsibility to defend with inadequate forces, most of them undertrained and poorly equipped. He dozed off uneasily. Shortly before 4:00 a.m. he was awakened by the phone.

General Richard Sutherland, MacArthur's replacement for Eisenhower as his Chief of Staff, said tensely, "General, the Japs are bombing Pearl Harbor."

"What!" Doug was incredulous. Then, recovering from his astonishment, he ordered his entire staff awakened immediately and told to report to his headquarters.

When he put the phone down, he remained lost in thought for a long while. It had happened at last. The crisis for which he had been preparing, and which he had warned was coming for over twenty years, had finally exploded in the faces of the astonished American people. His jaw set in a stern line, he picked up a Bible at his bedside and read it briefly.

Then he got into uniform and, as an afterthought, strapped on his sidearms. Doug MacArthur, hero of the Rainbow Division, was going into battle once more.

9

"I Shall Return"

Ten hours after the attack on Pearl Harbor, waves of Japanese planes swept over Clark Field on Luzon, sixty-five miles from Manila. Scorning the feeble ground fire of a few rusty antiaircraft guns, they bombed Luzon's one airfield so devastatingly that seventeen bombers and forty fighters were left burning wrecks, along with smashed supply depots and installations. In a few shocking moments MacArthur had lost half his air force. Worse, he had lost them in the most humiliating manner possible—on the ground, only hours after the warning of Pearl Harbor.

A fresh storm of criticism was unleashed in Washington, bitterly assailing MacArthur for having been caught "asleep at the switch," just like the admirals in Hawaii. Actually, a few days earlier he had ordered General Lewis H. Brereton to send their thirty-five bombers from Clark Field to the southern island of Mindanao. For reasons which have never become fully clear, Brereton dispatched only half the B-17s. MacArthur, in typical fashion, assumed full responsibility for the error which had given the Japs control of the air at one sharp stroke.

Nor did he reproach Brereton privately. "We'd have lost all our air power in a day or two anyway," he confided in Sutherland. "We're too weak in dispersal areas, ground defenses, and gas supplies, and the Japs have total air superiority."

On December 9th the Japs began making small amphibious landings in northern and southern Luzon. MacArthur's orders involved a strategy called the "Orange Plan," requiring him to fight holding actions while retreating slowly to Bataan Peninsula, then to the island fortress of Corregidor which commanded the entrance to Manila Bay, until the American Navy could come to his rescue. Doug had frequently assured the War Department that "Corregidor is the strongest, single fortified point in the world," because its concrete underground tunnel made it so impregnable to bombs and shells that it was known as "The Rock." Washington assumed that the MacArthur forces could hold off the Japs, and prevent the capture of Manila Bay, for four months. MacArthur was also convinced that Manila itself could be held for a long period. He was not the first great leader—nor would he be the last—whose predictions did not always support his legend of infallibility.

He correctly gauged the first Jap landings on Luzon as mere feints, however, designed to lure his forces out of position.

"Sit tight," he told General Jonathan "Skinny" Wainwright. "If I'm any judge of Jap strategy, they're going to throw everything at us at Lingayen Gulf. Get ready to mow them down on the beaches and in the water."

On December 12th an armada of 154 Jap ships steamed into Lingayen Gulf for a full-scale invasion. Wainwright was waiting for them. The first waves of infantry Japanese General Masaharu Homma threw at the beaches of Lingayen were blown to pieces in the water and on the mined sands. Artillery shells scored devastating hits on invasion barges and troop transports.

Chagrined and astonished, Homma withdrew his invasion fleet of two hundred thousand men to shape a new strategy. Twelve days later he poured men ashore on the north coast of Luzon, then returned again in force to Lingayen Gulf with a powerful cover of carrier-based fighter planes which swept the air and sea free of all resistance, and smashed all artillery positions zeroed in on the beaches.

"They've got us now, General," Wainwright phoned Doug.

"Hang on as long as possible, Skinny. Don't get caught in the Jap pincers, but slow them down every inch you can."

In Washington, meanwhile, General Marshall called in MacArthur's former Chief of Staff, "Ike" Eisenhower, for advice on Pacific strategy. Eisenhower agreed that the Philippines would have to be temporarily sacrificed in order to rush all of America's war production to Europe, North Africa, and Russia to stop Hitler and Mussolini. Australia could be set up as the chief base of Pacific operations, to be used later as the springboard for a counter-offensive against Japan.

Marshall nodded. "MacArthur will simply have to realize, besides, that since Pearl Harbor we just don't have the naval forces to help him hold on to the Philippines."

Doug angrily protested to Marshall that the Japs' sea blockade of the Islands was thin and easily punctured, but only negligible aid reached him in a few submarines. Roosevelt wired Quezon, "I give to the people of the Philippines my solemn pledge that their freedom will be redeemed and their independence established and protected." Both Quezon and MacArthur glumly understood they were being told to wait until victory in Europe.

Down in Australia, Prime Minister John Curtin also understood. Aware that Churchill had already written off the continent down under as "expendable," he protested bitterly, "I make it clear that Australia looks to America, free from any pangs about our traditional links of friendship to Britain. . . . We know that Australia can go and Britain still hang on. We are determined that Australia shall *not* go. . . . We refuse to accept the dictum that the Pacific struggle is a subordinate segment of the general conflict."

On December 26th Jap bombers flew over Manila Bay and unleashed a thunder of death and destruction on the surface installations of Corregidor. Visiting The Rock at the time, MacArthur stood erect on the lawn of an Army house, calmly watching bombs explode around him. His example of unruffled courage was not lost on the troops of Corregidor.

From his studies of Japanese strategy, Doug was certain that Homma expected him to make a last-ditch stand in Manila. Instead, he ordered his commanders to "side-slip" away from the capital into Bataan peninsula, exacting a heavy toll of enemy troops as they did. They were to join forces in a twenty-mile line across the neck of Bataan, and fight a fierce delaying action from swampy jungles and mountain strongholds. Manila, instead of being defended, would be declared an open city to save the lives of six hundred thousand Filipino civilians, and MacArthur would move his headquarters to rocky Corregidor.

So thoroughly did this plan upset Homma's calculations that the exasperated Commander of the 14th Japanese Army, in the words of official Japanese records, "could not adjust to the new situation." Homma's planes could not find MacArthur's troops in the thick jungles of the Bataan peninsula, where rain-flooded swamps also bogged down the invaders' tanks and troops. Filipino guerrillas harassed the Japs further from treetops, hurling down grenades as they swung Tarzan-like through groves of mahogany trees on parasitic *balete* vines. Hidden artillery and snipers paved the jungle with enemy dead. Bridges the Japs had counted on using to swarm into Bataan were blown up in their faces.

But MacArthur's defense of the peninsula was complicated by the fact that twenty-six thousand Filipino civilians had fled into Bataan along with Wainwright's retreating forces. Doug had stocked Bataan with only 150 days of rations for the troops.

"What should I do?" Wainwright demanded. "I can't let the civilians starve."

"Of course not. Put the whole command on half rations. Then, if you have to, quarter rations."

To spare Manila, MacArthur declared it an undefended open city. Hours later hordes of Jap bombers flew over the city, demonstrating Homma's contempt for the rules of war adopted by the Geneva Convention. Tons of explosives were dumped on churches, schools, colleges and hospitals, killing thousands of Filipino women and children.

Doug told Jean to pack the bare necessities needed for them, Arthur, and their son's Chinese nurse, Ah Chuh. It was time to leave for Corregidor, his new headquarters. As the door closed, Jean suddenly remembered something infinitely more precious than the clothing in one of her suitcases. She ran back into the apartment, dumped the clothing on the floor, and refilled the case with all the medals that had been awarded to her husband during the past forty-five years.

January on Bataan and Corregidor was a month of heartbreaking struggle and suffering. MacArthur's troops were decimated by malaria and tropical diseases, growing thin and weak with hunger and fatigue. Horses and mules had to be slaughtered for food. At headquarters inside the Malinta Tunnel of Corregidor, the air was chokingly foul. Manuel Quezon, who was there with MacArthur, suffered a severe attack of TB and could barely walk. The island fortress shook with the weight of daily bombings. When a direct hit was scored on Doug's slate-gray cottage—fortunately while no one was in it—he simply moved into another house.

One Jap bomber flooded the skies over Corregidor with propaganda in the form of an open letter to MacArthur from General Homma, and on the reverse side a message to Filipino troops. Homma called on Doug to surrender, telling him, "You are well aware that you are doomed. The end is near. The question is how long you will be able to resist. You have already cut rations by half. I appreciate the fighting spirit of yourself and your troops who have been fighting with courage. Your prestige and honor have been upheld. However, in order to avoid needless bloodshed and to save your 1st, 31st Divisions, and the remnants of other divisions . . . you are advised to surrender."

On the reverse side Homma told the Filipinos: "Unable to realize the present situation, blinded General MacArthur has stupidly refused our proposal and continues futile struggle at the cost of your precious lives. . . . Surrender at once and build your new Philippines for and by Filipinos."

Doug crumpled this leaflet in his hand and radioed a plea to all the men in his command to hold out for just a few months, by which time he promised them help would come. He sent daily messages to Washington begging for equipment, supplies, a few planes for reconnaissance, and a Navy assault on Jap positions as soon as possible.

Inspired by MacArthur and believing in him, American and Filipino defenders of the Islands fought their hearts out, stopping three huge onslaughts by the Japs. They had been holding back the enemy fifty days when Doug celebrated his sixty-second birthday on January 26, 1942. Roosevelt sent a special message to Corregidor: CONGRATULATIONS ON THE MAGNIFICENT STAND THAT YOU AND YOUR MEN ARE MAKING. WE ARE WATCHING WITH PRIDE AND UNDERSTANDING, AND ARE THINKING OF YOU ON YOUR BIRTHDAY.

When the message arrived, MacArthur was making the rounds of the forward command posts on Bataan. Over the roar of exploding shells around them, General Wainwright reproached him for not wearing a regulation steel helmet. Doug shrugged.

"Morale effect," he grinned. "The soldiers say, 'I guess if the Old Man can take it, I can, too!'" He told Wainwright that he was going to set up his own advance headquarters on Bataan.

Upon returning to the tunnel, he announced this decision to Quezon, who wrathfully protested that he had no right to risk his life when it meant so much to the Philippines. Quezon pointed out that the Filipinos knew and trusted only him personally, not the distant land called America, and that if he were killed they might begin to listen to Japanese promises of independence.

MacArthur hesitated, then reluctantly gave Quezon his word to make no further trips to the Bataan front. Anti-MacArthur officers—of whom there were never any great lack—quickly coined the slanderous term "Dug-out Doug" to suggest an image of MacArthur hiding in the tunnel of Corregidor, an obvious lie to any old soldier familiar with MacArthur's heroic war record.

As the Japs forced the Islands' defenders back in bloody fighting, Roosevelt wired MacArthur, "American forces will continue to keep our flag flying in the Philippines so long as there remains any possibility of resistance." But the President also suggested that Quezon's official party should leave for Australia by submarine, and that Jean MacArthur, little four-year-old Arthur, and the wife of High Commissioner Sayre should go along.

"I think you ought to leave, ma'am," Doug told Jean. "It may be the last chance. I know you'd rather stay here with me, but we've got to think of the little Sergeant."

Jean's soft hazel eyes held his. "The three of us are one," she said quietly. "We shall stay together and drink from the same cup. Don't send us away."

Proud but worried, Doug told Quezon of Jean's decision to "share the fate of the garrison." The leader of the Filipinos, now confined to a wheelchair, shook his head sadly as he prepared to board a Navy sub for Australia.

"You are signing their death warrant, Douglas," he sighed.

On February 15th Singapore fell, freeing the Japs to sweep through the Southwest Pacific. MacArthur knew that Tokyo would not endure much longer the humiliation of being frustrated by his token forces. The Japs had expected to take the Islands in eight weeks. By upsetting their timetable, Doug was gaining valuable time for Australia to be built up as the springboard for a counter-offensive. Premier Tojo began sending furious messages to General Homma, at the same time that fresh Jap troops were poured into Luzon until MacArthur's tattered, starved, but stubborn heroes of Bataan were outnumbered ten to one.

All of America drew inspiration from their obstinate, brilliant fight against overwhelming odds. At a Washington's Birthday banquet, veterans who had served with Doug saluted him by short-wave radio. Brigadier General James Crane called him "our loyal friend, who causes every American to say, 'There stands a man!'" Colonel "Wild Bill" Donovan described him as "a symbol for our nation—outnumbered, outgunned, with the seas around him and skies above controlled by the enemy, fighting for freedom!" Colonel John Monroe called out across the Pacific, "No matter to what heights you carry your fame, you will not astonish us—your old friends of the Rainbow Division. *Good luck, General MacArthur!*"

Doug did not doubt that he would die at Corregidor, either leading a final charge against Homma's troops or being blown to bits by Jap artillery or air raids. He was even steeled to the deaths of Jean and little Arthur. Never for a moment did he entertain the possibility of surrender.

It was something of a shock, therefore, when he received a personal radio message from the President to leave Corregidor as rapidly as possible for Australia to take command of a new Southwest Pacific Area. Doug was appalled at being asked to leave his men, and told General Sutherland that he simply couldn't obey the order.

"It would hurt the reputation of America through all of Asia," he explained. "Think of what Tokyo would say! The order is just plain wrong. It's like asking a captain to be the first off a sinking ship!"

"But, General, you *can't* disobey!" Sutherland argued. "This order comes from the President himself—your Commander-in-Chief—not just the War Department. They did that deliberately, don't you see, so you couldn't refuse!"

MacArthur fretted in a torment of indecision for two days. Finally he wrote Roosevelt that he would obey, but begged for a delay until a moment of his own choosing, to avoid the sudden collapse of Filipino resistance he knew would occur when Quezon's troops learned that he had left them. General Marshall replied for FDR, granting a brief delay.

But the cause was doomed. As Doug explained later, "The enemy was in overwhelming force. Filipinos fought well but were poorly armed. About a third of the reservists had but three months training, a third about two months, a third one month." Nevertheless, inspired by MacArthur, they resisted with such fanatical courage that on March 9th Tokyo radio announced that General Tomoyuki Yamashita, the tough conqueror of Singapore, was being sent north to crush the "foolishly stubborn troops on the Philippines."

The following day MacArthur received a blistering message from Washington. The President, irritated by Doug's reluctance to leave his men, ordered bluntly: "Leave immediately!" A submarine of the type that had taken Quezon to Australia was being made available. MacArthur refused it, announcing that he and his party would leave in PT boats, as though to show his defiance of Japanese control of air and sea in the Pacific.

Selecting the twenty people he was allowed to take with him, he admitted unhappily to Jean, was the hardest decision he ever had to make in his life. He knew those left behind would either die or suffer the torments of a Jap prison compound. Ah Chuh had to be taken because of the certainty she would be tortured to reveal everything she knew about the MacArthurs.

On the night of March 11th, four sixty-five-foot motor torpedo boats arrived at the bomb-blasted south dock of Corregidor. Doug helped Jean, Arthur, and Ah Chuh into one boat, while eighteen of his staff boarded the others. Then MacArthur, the last on the dock, looked slowly around the burned and blackened ruins of Corregidor as tears glistened in his eyes.

He held out his hand to General Wainwright, to whom he had turned over command of the doomed forces. "Goodbye, Jonathan," he said in a voice hoarse with emotion. "It's up to you now. Hold out as long as you can. If I get through to Australia, I'll come back as fast as I can with everything I can get—depend upon it!"

"I know you will, Doug," Wainwright said. "God bless you."

MacArthur embraced him and blurted, "I *shall* return!" Then he turned quickly and leaped into the lead PT boat.

"Cast off, Buck," he ordered tightly.

The seas were so heavy that night that Doug found it impossible to keep his feet. Japanese mine fields, and a sighting of Jap warships on a blockade patrol, forced the PT boats to separate in order to dash through the gantlet. MacArthur's boat ran out of fuel. They had to land at an island and transfer to another PT. Heading for Mindanao in daylight, they sighted a Jap cruiser angling toward them. The crew cut the engines and they waited helplessly for disaster. Luckily the enemy cruiser changed course without seeing them.

On the morning of the second day they reached Mindanao, where they waited three days for three Navy Flying Fortresses sent north to pick up the MacArthur party. Only two arrived, but these had to suffice because the Japs were aware that Doug was on Mindanao, and every moment's delay was risky. The MacArthur party was flown south for eleven hours over Jap-held air bases in the East Indies, Timor, and New Guinea.

On March 17th the planes touched down at Batchelor Field, forty miles south of Darwin in Australia's Northern Territory. They were greeted by an Australian general, who congratulated MacArthur on his last-minute escape from doomed Corregidor. Doug told him grimly, "I came through—and I shall return!"

Cars were produced to whisk the MacArthur party south to Alice Springs. Less than ten minutes after they had gone, Jap dive bombers and fighters roared over Darwin's airport in a furious attack. It was obvious that Japanese Intelligence knew where Doug was, and had launched a last desperate attack in an effort to kill the one American they feared most.

Told of the attack at Alice Springs, MacArthur shrugged.

"It was close, but that's the way it is in war," he said. "You win or lose, live or die—and the difference is just an eyelash."

But that eyelash was to cost Japan the war.

10

Year of the Impossible

Doug naturally assumed that during the valuable time he had gained for his country by stalling the Japanese war machine in Bataan and Corregidor, a large, trained military force had been assembled for him in Australia. En route to Melbourne by train across the vast desert wilderness of South Australia, he waited eagerly for the report of his deputy chief of Staff, General Richard Marshall, who boarded the train at Adelaide.

"Well, Dick, what sort of shape are we in?"

Marshall shook his head glumly as he delivered the bad news. There were only twenty-five thousand American soldiers in all of Australia, untrained and not even infantrymen, with less than a hundred serviceable planes. As for the Australian infantry, the only three seasoned divisions were away fighting in the North African desert.

MacArthur clenched his teeth until his jaws showed white.

"God have mercy on us," he muttered incredulously. Later he admitted, "It was the greatest shock and surprise of the whole war." He realized suddenly that Washington was simply using him as window dressing, counting on his fame and prestige to make it seem as though military strength was being built up in the Southwest Pacific. Far from having enough forces to go to the rescue of the Philippines, he had only a trickle of troops and equipment with which to defend the shores of Australia.

Turning to Jean beside him in the railroad car, he said bitterly, "Must I always lead a forlorn hope? They expect miracles of me, yet they rush the whole American war effort to Britain and Russia, and send me a shoestring."

Jean squeezed his hand comfortingly. "Poor Sir Boss! But somehow or other you'll manage to make Operation Shoestring work."

"Madam, I wish I had *your* confidence in your husband!"

Doubt and disappointment were still weighing heavily on his mind when his train pulled into Melbourne, and he was greeted by deafening cheers from an enormous crowd. An Australian general pumped his hand enthusiastically and shouted above the uproar, "Sir, this is worth twenty divisions to us!"

But when MacArthur spoke briefly to the thousands who had jammed the railroad station to welcome him, he refused to encourage false illusions. "I have every confidence in the ultimate success of our joint cause," he told them. "But success in modern warfare requires something more than courage and willingness to die. No general can make something out of nothing. My success or failure will depend primarily upon the resources which the respective governments place at my disposal. In any event, I shall do my best. I shall keep the soldiers' faith."

In Canberra, Australia's gleaming white capital city, Doug met the man who had asked Washington for him—slender, popular Prime Minister John Curtin, leader of the Labor Party. Despite MacArthur's own conservative political views, he warmed to Curtin instantly. Putting an impulsive arm around the Australian's shoulder, he said earnestly, "Mr. Prime Minister, you and I will see this thing through together." That night, at a banquet in his honor, he told Australia's leaders, "There can be no compromise. We shall win or we shall die."

Meanwhile, Doug's gallant fight in Bataan and Corregidor had so stirred the American Congress that they voted to award him the prize that had eluded him twice before—the Congressional Medal of Honor. President Roosevelt bowed to the wishes of Congress and bestowed the distinction upon MacArthur, who received it from the American Ambassador in front of the whole Australian Parliament. One of Doug's staff asked him afterwards how it felt to receive at last America's highest award, which it had taken him three wars to earn.

"Let's get on with *this* war," he replied dryly.

Valuable time was running out. The Japanese, flushed with triumph, were sweeping irresistibly southward. From Truk, their powerful naval and air base in the central Pacific, they seized and built up Rabaul on the northern tip of New Britain to serve as the major base for the assault on New Guinea and Australia. Early in March, 1942, a Japanese invasion force seized Lae and Salamaua, key ports and airfields in Papua, the Australian southern half of New Guinea. Across the Owen Stanley Range, forty-five minutes from Lae by bomber, was Port Moresby, last remaining obstacle between Japan and the invasion of the Australian continent.

On May 3rd a Japanese task force left Rabaul to invade Moresby. Knowing how much was at stake, MacArthur stayed up all night to follow developments as an American task force intercepted near Milne Bay. The Battle of the Coral Sea was fought entirely by carrier planes from the two fleets battering each other's ships. The Japs were so badly crippled that the task force turned back to Rabaul. Doug breathed a sigh of relief, knowing that Moresby was safe for a little while longer.

He redoubled his pleas to Washington for sufficient forces with which to return to the rescue of the Philippines. He had not forgotten the men on Bataan. But it was too late. On May 6th General Wainwright was forced to surrender the ten thousand troops on The Rock. The Japanese, furious at having had crack troops tied up in the Philippines for five months instead of the two they had expected, treated the survivors with savage cruelty.

The Americans were slapped, kicked, jeered at, starved, and medically neglected, with those who protested being bayoneted or beaten to death with gun butts. Prisoners were led on an infamous twelve-day trek to a prison camp, which became known as the "Bataan Death March" because so many Americans died of thirst or were killed for falling out of ranks because of exhaustion or illness.

When news of Bataan's fall reached MacArthur, his reaction astonished those associates accustomed to thinking of him as "a tough old codger." Head bowed in grief, his face remained a grim mask, but his cheeks were streaked with tears. He canceled all his appointments for the day, brooding behind closed doors. Reporters were not allowed to question him until the next day.

"The Bataan Force went out as it would have wished, fighting to the end of its flickering, forlorn hope," MacArthur finally told them. "No army has ever done so much with so little. Nothing became it like its last hour of trial and agony." After Corregidor fell a month later, he said grimly, "Corregidor needs no comment from me. It has sounded its own story at the mouth of its guns."

When he heard of the atrocities committed by the Japanese conquerors of the Philippines, through the report of three American soldiers who had escaped from Davao prison camp, he was shaken with anger as rarely before in his life. To avenge Bataan became an unswerving obsession.

"This unimpeachable record of savage and merciless brutality to captured prisoners of war fills me with unspeakable horror," he wrote bitterly in a statement prepared for the press. "It will become my sacred duty at the appropriate time to demand justice from those who have so barbarously violated all justice. God in His all-powering righteousness will surely punish the dreadful crimes visited upon the helpless officers and soldiers whom I had the signal honor to command in their noble and gallant struggle against overwhelming odds."

This statement was never released. According to Major General Courtney Whitney, one of MacArthur's aides, orders came from Washington the same day that news of Japan's war atrocities was to be withheld. "I am convinced," Whitney said later, "that this was because the 'Europe-firsters' then in power did not want an aroused public indignation to compel the diversion of a larger proportion of our military resources to the Pacific." Despite the genuineness of Doug's grief and anger, it may also be assumed that he was well aware that this consequence, so close to his military purposes, was a distinct possibility.

The Filipinos, who hated their Japanese conquerors, were quick to organize an underground resistance movement. MacArthur put Whitney in charge of directing the activities of the guerilla army, which also consisted of Americans who had escaped the Japs, reinforced by commandos brought in by subs. Whitney asked Doug for permission to use his public promise, "I shall return," as the inspirational slogan for the underground's propaganda campaign. MacArthur sent back the memo with a penciled notation: "No objections—I *shall* return. MacA."

This famous catchphrase was extraordinarily effective in keeping the spirit of Philippine resistance alive. But it brought a storm of bitter criticism down on Doug's head, particularly from Navy brass who wanted the slogan to read, "*We* shall return." MacArthur refused to change the message on cigarettes, matches, chewing gum, candy bars, sewing kits, and pencils, items in short supply smuggled into the Philippines. His refusal was seized upon as proof that he was "an egomaniac fighting his own personal war." But Doug simply looked upon the promise, "I shall return," as a personal pledge to the people of the Philippines as well as to his own imprisoned troops, and he knew that they had faith in that promise.

He did everything in his power to back up the guerillas. When they printed their own money, he promised that it would be redeemed at face value by the US after liberation. He smuggled field radios, ration kits, and signal flares to them by submarine, along with commandos to teach them sabotage, radio operation, and espionage. For two and a half years the underground drove the occupying forces mad with frustration, killing an estimated ten thousand Japanese and keeping Doug completely informed on Jap movements from 141 radio stations.

Radio intelligence from the Philippines was so thorough that MacArthur even knew which Japanese officers were staying at the Manila Hotel as soon as they registered. When told that Marshall Terauchi was occupying the suite where he and Jean had once lived, Doug observed dryly, "He should like it. It has a pair of vases given by the Emperor to my father in 1905."

One of MacArthur's first major problems in Australia was to resist and change the Australian Government's military thinking. Prime Minister Curtin explained that they expected him to yield the northern half of the continent to the Japs as largely empty and undefendable, building Australian defenses instead along a "Brisbane Line" which would protect the southeastern coastal cities of Brisbane, Sydney, Melbourne, and Adelaide, where most of the Australian population was concentrated.

MacArthur electrified both Canberra and Washington by rejecting the Brisbane Line plan, announcing that he intended to take the offensive instead. "We shall make the fight for Australia in New Guinea," he insisted. A holding operation in the south of Australia, he pointed out, would be "fatal to every possibility of ever assuming the offensive." His own daring plan was a gamble, and he knew that failure would be ruinous to both Allied hopes in the Pacific as well as to his own reputation. But from the moment he arrived in Australia he was convinced that only by carrying the war to the Japs in New Guinea could their preparations to invade the continent Down Under be thrown off-balance.

Australia's seven million people took new heart and hope from MacArthur's inspiring decision to attack. Their pro-American feeling became so strong that some Australians were even for withdrawing from the British Commonwealth after the war to work out some kind of ties with the United States.

To start his grand counter-offensive, Doug sought a unified command of land, air, and sea forces. One hand, he felt strongly, was necessary to coordinate all moves on the vast Pacific chessboard. But the Navy's admirals, still smarting over their humiliating debacle at Pearl Harbor, were determined to regain prestige by "running the show" against the Japs. Admiral Ernest J. King, Chief of Naval Operations, urged upon President Roosevelt a concept of the Pacific war as essentially an ocean operation which should be under Navy control. The result was an unsatisfactory compromise, with the Southwest Pacific continuing under MacArthur, while the Central Pacific command was given to Admiral Chester W. Nimitz. This split of authority often compelled Doug to support campaign strategy he disapproved.

Establishing his headquarters at Lennon's Hotel in semitropical Brisbane, one of his first acts was to shake up his tiny Air Force by sending for a new air commander from the States, General George C. Kenney. Reporting to MacArthur, Kenney was forced to listen to a scathing denunciation of the Air Force he was supposed to take over.

Kenney was not cowed by the MacArthur wrath. "I know how to run an Air Force," he snapped, "and I expect to be allowed to run my own show. Especially since you apparently had enough confidence in my ability to send for me!"

Doug's eyes twinkled. Throwing his arms around Kenney's shoulder, he said, "George, I think we're going to get along together all right!" His new air chief had passed the MacArthur test for spunk and generalship.

Kenney quickly proved himself a brilliant air commander who knew how to build up air power fast where it was needed. Once a newspaperman asked MacArthur where the Air Force's bombs were falling that day, and he replied, "In the right place—go ask George Kenney where it is!" Kenney's skill at using bombers to sink Jap shipping caused Doug to refer to him admiringly as "a twentieth century pirate," a tribute advertised by one Fifth Air Force bomb group who called themselves the "Jolly Rogers" and painted huge skulls on the tails of their Liberators.

Once, Kenney phoned MacArthur at 11:00 p.m. to report sinking a destroyer of a huge Jap convoy steaming south. Then he apologized for waking Doug up. "Don't apologize for news like that," MacArthur grinned sleepily. "Call me any time you can tell me that you are making some more Japs walk the plank." Kenney took him at his word and woke him at midnight to report another destroyer sunk; then again at 1:00 a.m., when he told Doug happily that a third Jap warship had been sunk and the convoy had turned back.

There was a contented snore at the other end of the line.

11

An Old Dog Learns New Tricks

Kenney became a good personal friend of the MacArthurs. He saw the human side of Doug, watching the man the Japs feared most march around his apartment each morning with little Arthur, both of them shouting, "Boomity, boomity, BOOM!" At the final "BOOM!" Arthur would cover his eyes while his father produced some tiny surprise. The gift Arthur treasured most was a miniature American flag—banner of the homeland he had never seen.

Jean MacArthur prepared all of Doug's meals personally, serving them at any odd hour he was ready to eat, and looked after him with a loving devotion that helped to account for his remarkable health and vigor at age sixty-three. Kenney marveled at Jean's skill in helping her husband relax from the heavy cares of command. "Someday," Kenney wrote later, "I hope that the world recognizes the important part Jean MacArthur played in winning the war in the Pacific."

In May 1942, MacArthur at last received some infantry troops—two untrained divisions, the 41st and 32nd, as well as some crack Australian brigades back from fighting in the African desert. Engineering officers reported that Port Moresby was not suitable for development into the offensive base Doug needed, so he immediately ordered construction of a base with airfields at a Lever Brothers coconut plantation in Milne Bay, at the southeastern tip of the island. Troops and equipment had to be ferried ashore by native outriggers. By June this jungle base, bombed daily by the Japs, was garrisoned by the 7th Australian Infantry Brigade, a company of the 46th US Engineers, and a squadron of RAAF P-40 fighter planes. Now Moresby's eastern flank was protected, and MacArthur had a new foothold in New Guinea from which to launch air attacks at the enemy. The Japs did not tolerate this threat long.

On July 22nd they landed large forces at Buna and Gona, wresting these lightly-held bases away from token Australian forces. This move put them only 100 miles from Moresby across the forbidding Owen Stanley Range, and about 160 miles northwest of Milne Bay. The battle was now joined. MacArthur had thrown down the gauntlet and the Japs had picked it up. The front lines were now in the jungle triangle formed by Moresby, Milne Bay, and Buna, and here the first major land clashes would take place.

The Japs moved first by sending five jungle-trained battalions up over the Kokoda Trail of the fourteen-thousand-foot Owen Stanlies, planning to spill down the other side and seize Moresby. A small Australian force at Moresby, outnumbered ten to one, nevertheless climbed their side of the Range, sweating and straining as they pulled field artillery pieces up the mountain by hand. They were pounded daily from the air by the Japs, who had complete command of the skies over New Guinea. At that time Kenney had only six B-17 bombers in combat condition. As for the American infantry, they were still being trained in jungle warfare in Queensland. The Aussies at Kokoda Pass fought bravely and desperately to hold the Japs back, but they were slowly forced to give ground in fierce mountain fighting.

This discouraging news added to morale problems of the first Americans sent to Moresby and Milne Bay. The average soldier was losing fifteen to twenty pounds a month from insufficient and bad food, dysentery, malaria, and blackwater fever. They fiercely resented not seeing the Supply Services, which they felt were too busy making things comfortable for headquarters and other rear echelon troops in Melbourne, Sydney, and Brisbane.

Acting on his old conviction that fighting men need to see their commander-in-chief sharing danger with them, MacArthur established a forward headquarters at Port Moresby, disdainful of the daily bombings and of the Jap infantry threatening to pour down from Kokoda Pass. He showed up in Moresby one morning, corncob pipe clenched between his teeth, and approached an astonished American soldier in fatigues. "Sergeant," he asked casually, "just how does the situation look to you?"

"Well, General," the sergeant stammered, "I'm just darn glad I've paid up my G.I. life insurance!"

The situation soon looked even blacker. On the night of August 25th, word was flashed to MacArthur that Milne Bay was about to be invaded by a convoy of Admiral Gunichi Mikawa's crack marines, who had never yet been successfully opposed.

"George, youve got to hit them with everything youve got that can fly!" Doug told Kenney grimly. "If that task force lands, we're in bad trouble." It was inconceivable that the invincible Japs could be checked by a handful of Australian infantry, and a few green companies of American engineers and air defense men, supported by a single squadron of Aussie pilots flying Kittyhawk fighters. Yet somehow Milne Bay had to be held, because three airstrips had just been completed there. If the Japs seized them they would be able to control the skies not only over Port Moresby, but also over Australia itself.

Kenney tried to sink Mikawa's invading force in Collingwood Bay, but foul weather kept his planes grounded during most of the crucial hours of the invasion. Jap marines and tanks poured ashore. Many of the American service troops, young and unseasoned, considered their last hours at hand and began reading their Bibles by the light of dawn as they waited with rifles and grenades in muddy slit trenches.

The stormy night which had protected the Jap convoy from Kenney's fliers also confused the invaders into landing short of their target, putting them ashore in a coastal quagmire several miles east of the Milne Bay base. This stroke of good fortune gave the Aussie infantry time to mount a small but bold counter-offensive. Clutching rifles and "Molotov cocktails"—explosives in bottles to hurl at tank treads—they plunged into the jungle in bare feet and undershorts, grinning and wisecracking with an utter disregard for danger.

Their courage amazed the Americans. "Those guys act like they're going on a picnic," one Ohio corporal marveled, "instead of to their own funeral!" But for twelve days the Australians fought with a skillful ferocity that astounded and confused the Japs, and led MacArthur to proclaim them among the finest—if not *the* finest—soldiers in the world. Daring Aussie pilots also flew Kittyhawks at treetop level, strafing the tops of coconut palms to kill Jap snipers tied to the branches. When Doug urged Kenney to bomb Jap positions with anything he had that could get into the air, Aussie fliers staggered aloft with bombs strapped to their fighter planes, and some even threw grenades out of ancient Tiger Moth trainers used as observation planes.

As often as the foul weather permitted, Jap airfields in Buna and Rabaul sent dive-bombers and fighters to pound and strafe the Milne Bay forces mercilessly. Every night Jap warships, including a cruiser, sent a thunder of screaming shells into Allied shore positions, and sank supply ships in the bay.

Fighting in the heavy tropical downpour, which turned jungle and swamp into a sodden morass, was a nightmare for both the Jap marines and Aussie infantry. They remained locked in grim combat until the Japs succeeded in landing a convoy of reinforcements, and broke through the lightly-armed Australians to attack the key airstrip. A first assault wave was driven off by an American anti-aircraft battery and two companies of American engineers, flanked by Aussie riflemen and mortar-men. On August 30th the Japs regrouped and made a second, all-out effort to capture the airstrip. But its defenders threw up such intense fire that not a single Jap was able to cross the strip alive. The astonished enemy, repulsed with heavy losses, with-drew at dawn with their dead left behind on the airstrip.

It was the beginning of the end for the badly battered inva-sion force. Jubilant Australians raced in pursuit of the retreating enemy as MacArthur ordered Australian General Sir Thomas Blarney to clear them out of the north shore of Milne Bay at once. Severe losses were suffered by both sides in savage hand-to-hand fighting. More Jap reinforcements were rushed toward Milne Bay, but clearer skies gave Kenney's pilots the chance they needed to sink and turn back convoy ships. Frustrated and enraged, Admiral Mikawa finally gave up and sent destroyers to Milne Bay at night to evacuate as many of the invaders as he could. His propaganda broadcasts, beamed at Allied troops in New Guinea, vowed revenge on "the bloody butchers of Milne Bay!"

But the Battle of Milne Bay was over, and it had ended in a stunning victory for Doug MacArthur, marking Japan's first land defeat of the war. The tide had begun to turn, and the proof that the Japs actually could be stopped sent morale soar-ing throughout the Southwest Pacific. There was more good news from the Kokoda Pass shortly afterward. Kenney, acting on MacArthur's orders, had used air power to knock out the Jap supply line between Buna and Kokoda. The exhausted, ragged, starved attackers finally bogged down only twenty-two miles from their goal. The Aussies counter-attacked, chasing them back over the Owen Stanlies to Buna.

With Moresby and Milne Bay secure, MacArthur jubilantly reversed gears and signaled for the start of his first offensive, aimed at the third corner of the crucial triangle—Buna. Now it was Japan's turn to go on the defensive. Jap forces at Buna worked furiously around the clock constructing a chain of underground pillboxes, each a miniature fortress with thick concrete and sheets of steel. Camouflaged coverings of logs, fifteen feet thick, protected them from shells and bombs. The approaches to these impregnable blockhouses were mostly swamps of black mud so deep they could drown a man. Major General Tomitaro Horii, in charge of the New Guinea infantry operation from Rabaul, was determined that he would break the back of Douglas MacArthur at Buna. It was here, indeed, that Horii lured Doug into making the worst mistake of his military career.

Unwilling to waste an unnecessary hour of his advantage, MacArthur ordered Kenney to fly the entire 32nd Division a thousand miles from their training center at Rockhampton, Queensland, to Moresby, and from Moresby over the Owen Stanlies to grasslands just south of Buna. Not only was this done, but Kenney's C-47 transports also flew in a complete army field hospital, including operating tables, to take care of casualties. MacArthur's success in this daring operation, despite fierce attacks by Jap fighter planes, marked the beginning of a new chapter of military history—flying an army into battle.

But this brilliant start was soon cancelled by six weeks of trying to inch through jungle swamp in what MacArthur's chief engineer called "the ultimate nightmare country." At the end of this time the men of the 32nd were a bearded, exhausted band in ragged uniforms, their shoes soggy, dilapidated sponges. Staggering from malaria, jungle rot, scrub typhus, dengue, blackwater fever, and "jungle guts" (tropical dysentery), they had no medical supplies with them and many died in the filthy mud where they dropped. They subsisted on a third of a C-ration and a couple of spoonfuls of rice a day, stumbling through a world of slippery muck caused by downpours that fell in sheets, bone-tired from pushing through neck-deep swamps. Their nights were spent in a sleepless fight against fierce mosquitoes, swamp rats, poisonous ants, ticks and chiggers, their days in tropical heat so blistering it caused jungle ulcers beneath their camouflaged "monkey suits" of green and brown.

By the time they reached the outer defenses of Buna on their approach march, they were so enfeebled by exhaustion, hunger, and disease as to warrant evacuation. But their officers, misled by faulty Intelligence reports from MacArthur's headquarters, assured them that Buna was only lightly held and could easily be taken. The men of the 32nd went into battle without a working field radio, without a single carbine, their weapons jammed by rain, muck, and dirt, with only two pieces of field artillery and no air support because of the relentless tropical rains.

They were stunned when enemy firepower cut them to ribbons from powerful concealed fortifications. Falling back in confusion, they desperately dug foxholes which immediately filled with water, but into which they burrowed nevertheless. Their commander, Major General Edwin Harding, desperately called for more ammunition and for an aerial pounding of the Jap positions. The ammunition was dropped by air, and bombloads were dumped on the thickly protected Jap forts, without the slightest effect. Then Colonel Hiroshi Yamamoto ordered his troops to counter-attack, and many demoralized, sick G.I.'s fled. After twenty-two days of continuous fighting against impossible odds and hellish conditions, half of the dazed, exhausted men of the 32nd were finally relieved. MacArthur's first offensive had failed.

Back in Moresby, the Supreme Commander paced the veranda of his headquarters looking grim and intense as he waited for the arrival of Lieutenant General Robert L. Eichelberger, whom he had summoned from Australia. When the tough infantry officer reported, Doug told him sharply, "Bob, I know that the 32nd hasn't been trained for jungle operations. I know that they're sick and that the climate is wearing them down. But a *real* leader could take these same men and capture Buna. You're to relieve Harding and do the job—or I will relieve them myself, and you, too!"

He warned Eichelberger that time was of the essence, because the Japs might land reinforcements any night. Then, continuing his restless pacing, he snapped, "Go out there, Bob, and take Buna—or *don't come back alive!*"

In the morning, feeling calmer and perhaps a little abashed by his strong language of the night before, he said, "Take good care of yourself, Bob, because you'll be of no use dead. There'll be a decoration for you, incidentally, if you take Buna. But remember, I must have Buna, regardless of casualties!"

Eichelberger promptly flew to the Buna front to inspect the situation before taking command. He demanded to know what changes General Harding was making in his staff to get things moving. "My commanders deserve to be decorated," Harding snapped angrily, "not relieved!" Eichelberger began to tongue-lash field officers of the 32nd, accusing them of coddling cowardice. He told them bluntly there would be no relief for the remaining half of the Division until Buna was taken.

"Eichelberger showed no appreciation of what the men had been through," General Harding noted bitterly in his diary as he turned command of the 32nd over to his successor. Eichelberger promptly ordered an all-out frontal attack on the impregnable enemy positions. The weary Americans stumbled forward in a new offensive, only to be cut down swiftly with terrible losses. Eichelberger, examining a captured Jap bunker, admitted in awe, "I hadn't realized what our troops were up against. It's easy to see now how the Japs held us up so long." One of his own staff officers, Colonel John E. Grose, vowed, "The 3rd Battalion's men have been courageous and willing, but they have been pushed beyond the limit of human endurance."

In the end Buna and Gona fell only when crack Australian troops mounted fierce flank attacks. At a terrible cost of 8,500

Yank and Australian casualties, the enemy strongholds were in MacArthur's hands by January 23rd. One year later over two thousand veterans of the Buna campaign had to be dropped out of the 32nd Division because they were still too ill to fight.

Three weeks after the Battle of Buna, MacArthur's headquarters issued a communique claiming that by not hurrying the attack, losses had been kept low, and that this had been possible because "the time element in this case was of little importance." This communique astonished Eichelberger, who had won the decoration Doug had promised him, but who had no intention of taking the blame for the expensive frontal assault on Buna.

"The statement that losses were small because there was no hurry was one of the great surprises of my life," he said bluntly. "Our Allied losses were heavy, and as commander in the field, I had been told many times of the necessity for speed."

Captured enemy documents at Buna also revealed that the Japs had not had regular food for a week, and had been reduced to subsisting on roots, grass, crabs, or snakes. "We were in such a position at Buna," admitted captured prisoner Major Mitsuo Koiwai, "that we wondered whether the Americans would bypass us and leave us to starve." MacArthur realized bitterly that if he had not been so determined to take Buna in a hurry by frontal attack, starvation would have given him the base in a few weeks without the loss of a single American or Australian soldier. The costly mistake weighed heavily on his heart.

He grimly determined that there would be no more disastrous frontal assaults on powerful Japanese positions. Learning from his blunder, he devised a whole new military strategy designed to save hundreds of thousands of American and Australian lives at the same time that it sped Allied victory. He now planned to "leapfrog" each strong Jap base, attacking and seizing instead a lightly defended enemy island north of it. He would then rush the construction of airstrips to pound the supply lines of the bypassed Jap troops, leaving them to "wither on the vine."

Using this technique he soon immobilized sixty thousand of the enemy at Hansa Bay, Wewak and Madang in northern New Guinea, frustrating and bewildering the Jap commanders there expecting his attack.

The angry outcry over his communique claiming "low losses" at Buna also made Doug sensitive to the importance of plausibility in battle reports. Not long after the Buna debacle fifty of Kenney's fighter planes ran into a formation of about the same number of Jap bombers and fighters. Displaying brilliant teamwork, the American pilots shot down ten Japs, scored ten more "probables," and damaged another five enemy planes—all, remarkably, without a single loss of their own planes. Kenney's joy turned to indignation when he read MacArthur's communique saying, "Our losses were light."

"Light!" Kenney protested in a shocked voice. "But, General, I didn't lose a single plane!"

"I know it, George. I want the communique to be accurate, but at the same time I want people to believe it. I think we'd better say our losses were light!"

12

Road Back to Bataan

The Japs first learned what MacArthur was up to when he bypassed their positions above Buna and Gona to invade the stronghold of Lae from the sea with an Australian division, at the same time dropping paratroops into the Markham Valley to seize the Jap airport at Nadzab twenty-five miles west. Despite the spluttering of his staff, Doug decided to fly in the lead plane to watch the first paratroop attack in the Pacific War.

"They're my kids, too," he told General Kenney firmly. "They'll be less scared knowing I'm right along with them."

"But it doesn't make sense!" Kenney protested. "After living all these years, and getting to be head general of the show, why is it necessary to risk having some five-dollar-a-month Jap aviator shoot a hole through you?"

"I'm not worried about getting shot, George. Honestly, the only thing that disturbs me is the possibility that when we hit the rough air over the mountains my stomach might get upset. I'd hate to get sick and disgrace myself in front of the kids!"

MacArthur's presence in the sky during the Nadzab paratroop attack squelched some Air Corps gossip that he was afraid of flying. Kenney knew these stories were baseless. Once he had awakened MacArthur on a B-17 flight to Moresby to tell him that an engine had conked out, but they were doing all right flying on three. Doug had grinned, "Nice comfortable feeling, isn't it?" Then he had gone back to sleep.

During the Nadzab operation an engine again quit on the bomber carrying MacArthur. The colonel in charge of the flight wanted to turn back to Moresby, but Doug wouldn't hear of it because Kenney had convinced him that a B-17 could fly almost as well on three engines as on four. The paratroop drop by the American Parachute Regiment caught the Japs off guard. "It was a honey!" Doug enthusiastically wired Jean in Brisbane.

With the airfield lost, the enraged enemy fell upon the amphibious Australian infantry wading ashore at Lae. MacArthur flew in more troops to attack the Japanese rear, and Lae was taken.

Doug's remarkable victories with token forces aroused such tremendous enthusiasm back home that a "We Want Mac" presidential boom began to sweep the country. Right-wing Republican supporters accused the Administration of failing to give MacArthur absolute command in the Pacific because of fear of his stature as a presidential possibility.

Toward the end of 1942 the political uproar grew so loud that Doug found it embarrassing and distracting. "I have no political ambitions whatsoever," he felt compelled to announce. "I started as a soldier and I shall finish as one."

Despite this disclaimer, a draft-MacArthur presidential boom continued to swell all during 1943. Many of those who persisted in pushing him forward as a candidate for the 1944 elections were isolationists and ultra-conservatives who, in General Kenney's opinion, "wanted to ride his coattails for their own interests more than his."

Doug had to keep assuring everyone that he had absolutely no interest in getting mixed up in politics. He even let President Roosevelt know this through Prime Minister Curtin, when the latter paid a visit to Washington. Curtin reported that FDR had been extremely happy at the news.

"I'm sure," the Australian laughed, "that every night when he turned in, the President had been looking under the bed to make dead sure you weren't there!"

Doug finally silenced all talk of his candidacy just before the Republican National Convention, when he sent word: "I request that no action be taken that would link my name in any way with the nomination. I do not covet it, nor would I accept it." The convention nominated Thomas E. Dewey instead.

MacArthur never let up in his pressure on Washington for more military aid to the Southwest Pacific theatre. Given only 2 percent of the total US Army and Air Force, and an even smaller percentage of the Navy, against an all-powerful enemy, it isn't surprising that he wrote bitterly to an old army friend: "I take some comfort from Stonewall Jackson's creed, 'that if necessary, we will fight them with sticks and stone.' But I find that sticks break in our hands and stones can't go very far."

One night at dinner with his staff, General Sutherland expressed the idea that democracy was a weak type of government in a national emergency, whereas military dictatorships were able to act swiftly and decisively. He implied that a vigorous dictatorship would not have been so slow and faltering in supporting MacArthur.

"No, Dick, you're wrong," Doug shook his head. "Democracy as we have it in the United States is the best form of government that man has ever evolved." After a thoughtful pause he added, "As long as a democracy can withstand the initial onslaught, it will find ways of striking back and eventually it will win. The trouble with you, Dick, I am afraid, is that you forget that we're fighting for the principles and ideals of a democracy."

Waging what his staff called "the poor man's war" on "Operation Shoestring," all through 1943 and 1944, MacArthur scored one brilliant victory after another. Because he always liked to "hit em where they ain't," casualties among his troops were the lowest of any theatre of war. In contrast, the Marines lost heavily in frontal assaults on Guadalcanal and other heavily-fortified islands held by Japs in the Central Pacific.

During the first week in March, 1943, a huge Jap convoy left Rabaul for New Guinea to bring reinforcements and food for the twenty thousand troops already there. Doug ordered Kenney to throw every plane in the Fifth Air Force at the heavily-escorted twenty-two-ship convoy. For three days American planes delivered a shattering air attack that sank almost every ship, and left only eight hundred Japanese survivors.

The Battle of the Bismarck Sea, as this great American air victory was called in MacArthur's communique, was a stunning defeat for the Japs. They no longer dared send any further expeditions south of Rabaul, conceding MacArthur's control of the air over New Guinea and the Bismarck Sea.

Doug was delighted with his fliers, and strongly approved of Kenney's policy of giving crews leave in Sydney, where their behavior was often, understandably, of the "eat-drink-and-be-merry-for-tomorrow-we-die" variety. A Service of Supply general stationed in Sydney complained indignantly to Kenney, "It's time those brats grew up and behaved themselves!"

The air chief saw red. "I have no desire to see them grow up into sedate, stodgy supply troops," he said between closed teeth, "because then they wouldn't be able to shoot down any more Nip planes or sink any more Nip boats!"

"Exactly," said a deep voice from the doorway. Kenney turned to see MacArthur standing there. Doug told the rear echelon general icily, "Leave Kenney's kids alone. I don't want to see them grow up either!"

Early in 1943 MacArthur wanted the US Joint Chiefs of Staff to approve of a swift seizure of Rabaul before the Japs could build it up into a great bastion of strength. But this recommendation had been ignored until the enemy forces on Rabaul were so powerful that any attempt to take it would have entailed heavy casualties. So MacArthur decided to bypass and neutralize Rabaul, and worked out a plan with Admiral William F. "Bull" Halsey whereby Doug's forces would spear up from New Guinea, and

Halsey's South Pacific forces from the Solomon chain of islands, for a surprise seizure of the lightly-held Admiralty Islands at the northern prong of the wishbone.

The dismayed Japs, who had expected MacArthur to continue fighting up the east coast of New Guinea, and then to assault Rabaul where fifty thousand Jap troops were expecting a crucial battle, were caught flatfooted by the coordinated attack. They hadn't dreamed MacArthur would dare take such a long leap upward toward the Philippines, leaving so many Jap bases at his rear. Equally astonished were the US Joint Chiefs of Staff, who had been told nothing of the plans for the Admiralty operations.

On February 29, 1944 MacArthur went ashore with Admiral Thomas C. Kinkaid at Los Negros, less than three hours after American troops hit the beach. Wet, cold, and dirty with mud up to his ears, Doug ignored the snipers' bullets whizzing from tall grass all around the island's coral airstrip. He was indifferent to the fact that his tall figure in a trench coat and field marshal's cap made him a prize target, and calmly walked around studying the military situation as it developed.

"Excuse me, sir," a nervous officer stammered, tugging him away from a large hut toward which he had been heading, "but we killed a sniper in there only a few minutes ago."

"Fine," MacArthur said. "That's the best thing to do with them."

In nine days the American flag was fluttering unchallenged over the Admiralties. At one brilliant stroke MacArthur had placed himself astride the supply lines of all Jap forces in the Solomons and New Guinea, leaving them behind to wither on the vine. He had advanced the timetable of the Pacific War by many months, saving thousands of Allied lives, and winning a US Naval Base almost as far north as the Equator.

Leapfrogging his forces up the long northern coast of New Guinea, Doug made the whole huge island his. In September 1944, advance headquarters were established in Hollandia, from which he directed the capture of Wake Island, Biak, Noemfoor,

Sansapor, and Morotai. MacArthur was understandably jubilant. He had fought back two thousand miles on the road to Corregidor in a little over two years, with fewer losses than the Allies had sustained at the single battle of Anzio Beach in Italy. And now, only three hundred miles to the north, lay the southern Philippines.

"I shall return!" he had sworn solemnly, and the keeping of his vow was at hand. It was for this high purpose that he had named every headquarters on the way back "Bataan," every Army phone exchange "Corregidor." But on the very threshold of his greatest triumph, a bitter surprise was in store for him. He was suddenly ordered by General Marshall to attend a mysterious conference in Hawaii with a "Mr. Big."

Flying to Pearl Harbor, Doug discovered that "Mr. Big" was President Roosevelt, who was being advised by the Joint Chiefs of Staff to bypass the Philippines and seize Formosa instead. The Hawaii conference had presumably been called to give MacArthur a chance to defend his Philippine strategy before FDR's definite decision. Stunned and dismayed, Doug suspected that the Navy's views had already prevailed, and that the President was simply using the conference for a pretext of impartiality. General Marshall had already hinted to MacArthur, "We must be careful not to allow our personal feeling and Philippine political considerations to overrule our great objective."

After dinner in a mansion overlooking Waikiki Beach, FDR asked Admiral Nimitz to state the Navy's case. Nimitz did so with great skill. Then Doug countered with the Army's view, emphasizing that a frontal assault on Formosa, without first taking the Philippines, would cost a fearful toll in lives. When he sat down he was grimly convinced that his cause was lost. So was Admiral Ernest King, FDR's chief naval adviser, who confidently took a plane back to Washington without even waiting for the President to announce his decision.

Anguished, Doug managed to see Roosevelt in private for a few minutes. "Mr. President," he said in a husky voice, "if you decide to bypass the Philippines and leave its millions of wards of the United States, and thousands of American internees and prisoners of war, to continue to languish in their agony and despair, I dare to say that the American people would be so aroused that they would register complete resentment against you at the polls this fall!" Voice choked with anguish, he rose to leave.

"Wait a minute, Douglas—come back here!" Roosevelt looked up at him with a quizzical grin. "You win. We're not going to bypass the Philippines. Carry out your existing plans, and may God protect you. Meanwhile, I'm going to have the devil of a time over this with that old bear, Ernie King!"

The President asked Doug to stay an extra day with him, and they talked of old times. The two men parted with warm handshakes, never to meet again. Doug was saddened by Roosevelt's obviously ailing health. Returning to Jean in Australia, he told her, "The President will be dead within six months." He was wrong by two months.

MacArthur set mid-November as D-Day for invasion of the Philippines, with the southernmost island of Mindanao as the initial target. However, a Navy pilot shot down over Leyte, and rescued by Philippine guerillas, returned to his carrier with the guerillas' report that there were small enemy forces and few planes stationed on Leyte. MacArthur and his staff decided to leap-frog Mindanao, invade Leyte with only light losses, and speed up reconquest of the islands by three months.

Kenney's bombers pounded Mindanao to mislead the enemy, and also cripple his air power, while MacArthur's headquarters radioed guerillas in the islands to spread rumors that the Americans would land in Mindanao. Doug grinned as Intelligence reports showed the Japs frantically strengthening Mindanao's defenses. But Kenney was worried, pointing out to MacArthur that they were seriously short of both troops and ships.

Doug still insisted that the invasion of the Philippines would take place—and a month ahead of schedule. "I tell you I'm going back there this fall," he assured his air chief, "if I have to paddle a canoe with you flying cover for me with that B-17 of yours!"

On October 16th a 650-ship convoy carrying 150,000 American troops left Hollandia, dodging a nearby typhoon which whirled past. Aboard the cruiser *Nashville* with Kenney and Sutherland, Doug woke on the morning of the 20th to the rumble of naval bombardment. Pushing aside the open Bible he had fallen asleep with, he dressed and went on deck. Leyte Gulf lay ahead beneath great rolling clouds which were thinning away to the horizon as the dawning sun banished them. Doug watched the *Nashville* dodge two floating mines, and saw two destroyer escorts dash after an enemy periscope with a battery of depth charges.

Returning below with General Whitney, he prepared to go ashore on one of the landing barges. Whitney watched quizzically as Doug slipped an old-fashioned revolver into his trouser pocket. "That belonged to my father," MacArthur explained. "I take it along to make certain I'm not captured alive."

Calmly smoking his corncob pipe to conceal his deep emotion, Doug waded ashore at "Red Beach" while shells and rockets were still shrieking overhead and carrier planes sent huge black mushrooms sprouting into the early morning sky. At his side was Sergio Osmena, the man who had succeeded to the presidency of the Philippines upon the death of the ailing Quezon, three months earlier.

Snipers' bullets whined over the dry coral sand, but Doug paid no attention. He was too absorbed in the sacred moment of standing again on Philippine soil, from which he had been driven two and a half years before. "Well," he murmured to Osmena, "we're back as we promised in March of 1942. It makes me sad that Manuel didn't live to see it."

Then gazing northward in the direction of Corregidor, he could not keep a quaver out of his voice as he added, "They are waiting for me there. It has been a long time."

Wearing his old Philippine Marshal's cap, and looking as though twenty years had dropped off his sixty-four, Doug walked into a palm grove to watch his troops fight their way inland. Pausing behind two soldiers who were firing from behind adjacent trees, he was noticed by one of them. The G.I. yelled to his friend in astonishment, "Hey, look! It's General MacArthur!" The other soldier sighted along his rifle and squeezed the trigger, without bothering to look around.

"Oh, sure it is," he drawled. "And I suppose he's got Eleanor Roosevelt along with him, huh?"

A radio transmitter was set up on the beach to spread the word through the secret radio network operated by Philippine guerillas. Broadcasting a dramatic appeal to the Filipinos to rally to him and help him throw out the invader, Doug's voice was choked with solemn emotion.

"This is the Voice of Freedom, General MacArthur speaking. I have returned. By the grace of Almighty God our forces stand again on Philippine soil. . . . At my side is your President, Sergio Osmena. . . . The hour of your redemption is here . . . Rally to me! Let the indomitable spirit of Bataan and Corregidor lead on. As the lines of battle roll forward to bring you within the zone of operations, rise and strike! For your homes and hearths, strike! For future generations of your sons and daughters, strike! In the name of your sacred dead, strike! Let no heart be faint. Let every arm be steeled!"

The alarmed war lords in Tokyo sped General Tomoyoki Yamashita, conqueror of Singapore, to Manila to defend Leyte and Luzon and slow down the Allied advance toward Japan. "The Tiger of Malaya" decided to fight it out at Leyte. He rushed reinforcements, dropped suicide squadrons of paratroops to infiltrate the American lines, and used what was left of the

Imperial Navy in a desperate attempt to sweep MacArthur's forces off the beaches of Leyte.

The fighting became ferocious. Despite his anxiety to take Leyte and go on to Corregidor, Doug let Yamashita slow him down rather than defeat him swiftly at a bloody cost. "I can finish Leyte in two weeks," he said grimly, "but I won't. I have too great a responsibility to the mothers and wives in America. I will not take by sacrifice what I can achieve by strategy."

He continued to walk about the front lines with his usual disregard for flying bullets. Once a Jap tank suddenly appeared, heading toward him, but was promptly hit and set afire by artillery. On the same day a Jap sniper was shot out of a tree seventy-five yards away from him. Kenney, who was with him at the time, sighed. "I'd feel happier inspecting this place from the air."

Doug laughed. "George, I think it's good for you to find out how the other half of the world lives!"

American troops fought their way into Tacloban, and MacArthur lost no time in setting up an advanced headquarters. Because only one captured airfield was usable, and that could handle only a few fighters, the skies over Leyte were filled with Yamashita's planes. One Jap pilot strafed MacArthur's headquarters, putting bullet holes in the wall inches from his head. An alarmed aide rushed in to find him calmly working at his desk.

"I'm not dead yet," Doug smiled. "But thanks for taking the trouble to check." Then he went on with his preparations to install Osmena as President of the Philippines in a formal ceremony.

The Japanese High Command sent three entire fleets into the waters around Leyte in a desperate gamble to smash the American Navy. One fleet lured Admiral Halsey's squadron from the San Bernadino Strait, so that a second fleet could enter Leyte Gulf, destroy two hundred American vessels at anchor, and then bombard MacArthur's shore positions to pieces.

The Japanese Central Fleet, under Admiral Kurita, sank a light American carrier and two destroyers, and drove Doug's troops out of their shore positions. MacArthur's staff brought the bad news to him with colorful opinions of Admiral Halsey for having left them vulnerable to Kurita's attack by chasing off after the Jap fleet that had served as a decoy force.

Doug pounded his desk angrily. "That's enough!" he commanded. "Leave the Bull alone. He's still a fighting Admiral in my book!" The whole Philippines campaign was now in jeopardy as a result of Halsey's mistake, but MacArthur would not tolerate criticism of an American officer whose blunder could only be attributed to an excessive fighting eagerness to engage and destroy the enemy.

13
"Show Him Where to Sign!"

MacArthur's ships and beachheads in Leyte Gulf now lay at the mercy of Admiral Kurita's shells and carrier bombers. But incredibly, Kurita didn't realize this and cautiously ordered his Japanese Central Force to retreat to the north, a blunder of even greater magnitude than Halsey's. This reprieve from the sea was quickly overshadowed by a fresh menace in the sky.

The flash and smoke of bomb bursts around the clock kept Doug's troops diving for slit trenches when they weren't frantically trying to re-build blown-up installations. Sleepless and haggard after two days under saturation bombings, MacArthur watched raids on ships in the harbor through binoculars. His jaw dropped in astonishment as he saw one Jap plane after another dive down through black puffs of anti-aircraft to crash deliberately onto the deck of an American ship. The harbor was filled with violent crimson explosions.

"My God, George," Doug muttered. *"Kamikazes!"*

They were witnessing Japan's first use of suicide planes, with pilots chained in the cockpit to keep them from panicking at the last moment and bailing out before plunging their bomb-laden aerial hearses into an embrace of death with the enemy.

Kenney shook his long thin head. "What kind of barbarians order their fliers to destroy themselves, without even the slightest chance of survival?"

"It's an admission of desperation," Doug said thoughtfully. "Tojo knows he's got to stop us here or he's through!"

A new and different roar overhead made both men peer into the skies to the south. MacArthur refocussed his binoculars, but even before he could identify the new planes Kenney's ears had told him whose engines they were hearing.

"Yippee!" he shouted. "It's my P-38's!"

"Thirty-four," counted Doug. "Come on, George, let's get down to the airstrip and give the kids a big welcome!"

Shaking hands with each awe-struck pilot, the Supreme Commander patted him on the back and told him fervently, "You don't know how glad I am to see you!"

With a small but effective air umbrella overhead, MacArthur was now free to make his decisive move against General Yamashita, who was building up his forces at the other end of Leyte for a huge counter-offensive. One morning the Tiger of Malaya was chagrined to find an American amphibious force suddenly pouring ashore at Ormoc in his rear. Before he could regroup his army, it was split in two. Fierce battles raged through most of December, but by Christmas Leyte was firmly in MacArthur's hands. Battering down the back door of the Philippines had cost 2,900 American lives, with almost ten thousand wounded. But the battle for Leyte had cost the Japanese an appalling toll of over fifty-six thousand dead.

A few days later Doug was wearing a new mark of distinction—the five stars of a General of the Army.

As 1945 dawned on the horizon of a war that had been blazing over the Pacific for three years, MacArthur lost no time in mounting an invasion of Luzon itself. On January 2nd he stood impatiently on the deck of a warship leading a convoy out of Leyte Gulf. Steaming north, they were incessantly attacked for four days by furious waves of *kamikazes,* which crashed into and sank thirty US transports and warships.

The convoy bulldozed through stubbornly, landing at Lingayen Gulf 110 miles north of Manila on January 9th, and pouring seventy thousand G.I.s ashore. Yamashita, now in Manila to direct the defenses of Luzon, was enraged. By various deceptive tricks MacArthur had led him to believe that the American landings would be made in the south of Luzon, and thus was able to strip the north of the island of two Jap divisions which were sped to Bataan.

Doug's plan was ingenious. Knowing that Yamashita would promptly rush his army north against the G.I. force at Lingayen Gulf, he planned to make a second invasion of the unguarded south, cutting off Yamashita's supply line. Both jaws of the American vise would crush the enemy between them, and the Philippines would be free.

His plan succeeded brilliantly. MacArthur advanced with his troops as they pressed southward under heavy fire. His corncob pipe under the faded field marshal's cap was a familiar sight in the front lines, and he seemed to be everywhere at once. He urged his line officers to advance with almost reckless speed to seize Manila.

"There are five thousand men, women and children prisoners in and around the city," he told them. "Intelligence reports show that our landing has turned the prison guards brutal. Unless we free the prisoners quickly, most of them may die."

Worried that he might be too late to prevent this tragedy, Doug remembered a bold tactic that had been used in the Civil War. He selected 134 commandoes who, aided by veteran Filipino guerillas, raced through and behind the Japanese lines. In a series of four daring surprise raids, they overwhelmed prison guards at compounds in Santo Tomas University, Bilibid, Cabanatuan, and Los Banos, freeing Allied prisoners at a cost of only two G.I's killed, ten wounded.

When MacArthur reached Manila with his troops, he was mobbed by thousands of weeping, shouting prisoners who tried to kiss his hand or touch his sleeve. At a military prison in Bilibid, he found many of the soldiers he had had to leave behind at Bataan and Corregidor. He was shocked to the point of tears at their wretched condition, many of them almost skeletons. Passing among them as they swayed at attention, he could only mutter hoarsely, "I'm long overdue, long overdue!" A ragged major who had fought at Bataan mumbled an apology for his unmilitary appearance. Doug gripped his hand fervently, and with deep emotion said, "Major, you never looked so good to me!"

Bombs and artillery shells thundered eight miles east of Manila as MacArthur installed Osmena as President of the Philippines at the Malacanan Palace on February 27th. "God has indeed blessed our arms," he told Osmena before a huge crowd of grateful Filipinos. "My country has kept the faith."

On March 2nd he returned to Corregidor the same way he had left in 1942—by PT boat. His heart heavy with poignant memories, he walked slowly around the Rock that had been the goal and symbol of his long struggle back. Late that afternoon, at a brief ceremony to indicate to the world that America had redeemed its honor, he said, "I see the old flagpole still stands. Haul the colors to its peak—and let no enemy ever haul them down!"

As soon as the last pockets of fanatical Japanese resistance had been wiped out in Manila, Doug sent for the two people he longed for most—Jean and little Arthur, neither of whom he had seen for six months. He could scarcely wait for the ship bringing them from Brisbane to the tropical city where Jean had once chosen to die at his side, rather than escape without him. After they had embraced on the dock, Doug placed a new jeweled watch around Jean's wrist. It was inscribed reverently, "To My Bravest."

Several groups of American planes roared overhead on their way to attack Jap positions in the hills. Jean turned to Kenney, who also had come to the dock to meet her, and said enthusiastically, "Isn't it wonderful to see *our* airplanes? The last time I was here, they were all Japs and instead of watching them we were running for cover. But, George, what have you done to Corregidor? I could hardly recognize it when we passed it this morning. It looks as though you had lowered it at least forty feet!"

"We might have, at that," Kenney grinned. "We unloaded four thousand tons of bombs on it in ten days before we took it!"

Doug, Jean, and Arthur moved into a house in the suburbs of Manila. A few days later they paid a visit to the ruins of their old penthouse apartment on top of the Manila Hotel.

"Oh, Doug, your library—it's ruined!" Jean was appalled at the mess. "So are all your scrapbooks! Oh, dear, the baby grand is burned out, and all the china is in pieces. And there's not a trace of the family silver!" Unexpectedly, the locked chest of silver showed up under the arm of a houseboy who had once worked for the MacArthurs. He had purloined it from the Japanese General who had seized it as personal booty, and had hidden it under rubbish in a cellar to await Doug's return. Because it bore the name of Arthur MacArthur, he was under the illusion that the chest contained the ashes of Doug's father.

Jean's presence in Manila angered many service wives back in the United States, who understandably also wanted to be reunited with their overseas husbands. According to one source, Washington made this unofficial reply to complaints: "If feminine companionship serves in any way to help MacArthur, let her stay there. MacArthur is not a young man. Maybe he needs his wife." It was, perhaps, a small enough concession for a sixty-five-year-old General of the Army who had shared the mud, rainstorms, bullets, and bombs with boys young enough to be his grandsons; who had led them all the way back to Bataan, in eighty-seven different major amphibious landings, never once permitting them to be pushed off any island or atoll they invaded.

When MacArthur completed mopping-up operations three months later, and the Philippines were declared liberated, his name rang around the world in paeans of extravagant praise. He had retaken more territory, with less loss of life, than any commander in history. What was even more amazing was that he had done this on the offensive against a fanatical enemy resolved to die rather than surrender. MacArthur had cost the Japanese almost half a million dead, with another quarter million men bypassed to "die on the vine," at a price of eight thousand American lives. The lesson he had learned at the debacle of Buna had been a hard one, but he had learned it brilliantly.

In tragic contrast, Admiral Nimitz's forces in the Central Pacific suffered twenty-four thousand casualties during the Marine invasion of toughly defended Iwo Jima, a strategically crucial two-by-four-mile island south of Japan. The naval command's invasion of the island of Okinawa, the next stepping stone to Japan itself, cost another forty thousand casualties between April and June. MacArthur was highly critical of such costly direct assaults, which he felt could have been avoided by imaginative leadership aware of how to use surprise amphibious landings and the dropping of paratroops behind enemy lines.

Meanwhile other historic events were happening during this same spring. On April 12th President Roosevelt died, to be succeeded by the man who had once been an artillery captain in MacArthur's Rainbow Division, Vice President Harry S. Truman. Less than a month later, on May 8th, Nazi Germany surrendered, releasing the full might of the Allies to turn against Tokyo. Japan was already being heavily bombed by long-range B-29's, and shelled by Admiral Halsey's Third Fleet.

The US Joint Chiefs of Staff set November 1st as the target date for "Operation Olympic," the invasion of Japan, with MacArthur leading the Army and Nimitz the Navy. The War Department was afraid that the Japanese would hold out for another two years, unless the Russians were brought into the Pacific war to clear them out of Manchuria, which would then entitle Stalin to share in the postwar occupation of Japan.

MacArthur knew the hopelessness of the Japanese position, and was aware that through secret diplomacy Tokyo was trying to get Moscow to arrange a Japanese surrender that would permit Emperor Hirohito to stay on his throne. In July Doug confided to Kenney, "I'm working on the plans for Operation Olympic, but I'm sure it will never take place. I predict that the Japs will capitulate next month, or even sooner."

Appealing to MacArthur's appreciation of psychological warfare, the O.S.S.—Office of Strategic Services, known as "the cloak-and-dagger boys"—suggested to him that just before American troops invaded Japan, several hundred foxes daubed with phosphorescent paint should first be splashed ashore. This would help spread consternation and panic among the superstitious Japanese who believed "a ghostly fox seen at night carries an evil spirit." Doug pointed out that the swim ashore would wash off most of the phosphorus. To prove he was wrong, the O.S.S. tried the scheme out in Chesapeake Bay. When the foxes swam ashore, most of the paint was gone, and the little that was left was promptly licked off by the animals on the beach.

In June, as a diversion, MacArthur went ashore with an assault wave of Australian troops sent to capture Borneo and cut off oil shipments to Japan. A press photographer trying to take his picture was hit by a bullet meant for Doug, who pressed inland with the Aussies through heavy rifle fire. On top of a hill an Australian brigadier handed him a map, pointing out various military objectives. A machine gun began raking the hill, and the two men's aides hit the earth, sliding backwards down the slope. MacArthur listened calmly as the Australian general continued their unperturbed discussion. Then, handing the map back, he suggested casually that they visit another hill to see what was going on there.

"By the way," he added, "I think it might be a good idea to have a patrol take out that Jap machine gunner before he hurts someone." As the fighting grew hotter, Kenney grew increasingly nervous about MacArthur's disregard of safety. He finally hit upon the ruse of urging Doug to return to their cruiser in order not to be discourteous to the captain of the *Boise* by keeping him waiting for his dinner guests, especially since the captain had promised to serve chocolate ice cream.

"All right, George," Doug smiled, "I wouldn't have you miss that ice cream for anything!"

Forty-eight hours before the dawn of the Atomic Age, MacArthur was told by a general from Washington that the world's first A-bomb would explode over Hiroshima on August 6th. Doug was surprised, as he was convinced that this extreme step was not needed to bring Japan to her knees. He suspected that the decision was a political one, designed to hasten a Japanese surrender before the Soviet Union could enter the war, as well as to justify the expenditure of two billion dollars on the Manhattan Project, which had developed the A-bomb.

When this terrible weapon fell out of the skies over the city of Hiroshima, it killed over seventy-eight thousand Japanese men, women, and children, with another forty-eight thousand injured or missing. President Truman warned grimly that if Tokyo did not surrender, Japan could expect "a rain of ruin from the air, the like of which has never been seen on this earth." The following day, before Tokyo could sue for terms, the Japanese ambassador in Moscow was called to the Kremlin and handed a Soviet declaration of war. Then, on August 9th a second A-bomb dropped on Nagasaki, leaving another seventy-four thousand dead beneath its mushroom cloud.

"This is it!" MacArthur told Kenney grimly.

Japan sued for peace the next day, and on August 13th Emperor Hirohito went on the radio to tell his people that they had lost the war, and should stop fighting. He had to flee and hide in a bomb-proof shelter to save himself from a thousand infuriated soldiers who broke into the palace. The following evening Truman broadcast his acceptance of "the unconditional surrender of Japan," and announced that Britain, China, and Russia had agreed to the appointment of MacArthur as Supreme Commander for the Allied Powers (SCAP).

Navy brass was outraged, and Jean was delighted. "Yes," she told her husband, "you really *are* Sir Boss now!"

MacArthur lost no time in letting the Japanese know it. He radioed Tokyo to send a delegation promptly to Manila for surrender instructions, and to use the call letters B-A-T-A-A-N to identify their plane. The Japs radioed back that they would come as soon as possible, and would use the call letters J-N-P. MacArthur sternly replied that they would come *immediately,* and the call letters would be B-A-T-A-A-N . . . or else! When the sixteen-man Japanese delegation arrived, he refused to see them, turning them over to his staff, who gave them twenty-five pages of orders.

Doug stunned his staff by announcing his intention to fly into Atsugi airdrome near Yokohama with just a few aides and a handful of troops. They begged him to wait until General Eichelberger first moved occupation forces into Japan. The country was still an armed hostile camp, with 2,500,000 home troops dangerously uncertain whether to obey the Emperor or the fanatical War Party plotting to seize power and continue the war.

"My God, General," Chief of Staff Sutherland fumed, "the Emperor is worshipped as a real god, yet they still tried to assassinate him. What kind of a target does that make *you?*"

"I won't deny that what I'm doing is something of a gamble, Dick," MacArthur admitted, "But I know the Japanese mind, and nothing impresses them like a show of absolute fearlessness. If they don't know they're licked, this could convince them."

Doug's staff didn't feel any easier learning that Atsugi Airfield was the base of three hundred Jap naval *kamikazes* who flew over Toyko dropping leaflets vowing to fight to the bitter end, no matter what the Emperor said, and urging popular support.

On August 30th the unarmed *Bataan* winged through the skies past Mt. Fujiyama in the west, with two B-17's as escorts. Awakened from a doze just before it was time to land, Doug requested his aides to leave all pistols behind in the planes. "There will be fifteen armed Japanese divisions a mile or two away," he pointed out. "If the Japs don't really mean what they said about surrendering, what good are a few pistols?"

Recalling the event six years later, Kenney said, "A number of Japs told me afterward that the sight of all those generals and officers of MacArthur's staff walking around unarmed in a country of seventy million people who only a few days before were enemies, made a tremendous impression on the Japanese. It told them more than anything else that they had lost the war."

A news flash from London brought an opinion from Winston Churchill, rugged wartime leader of the British, who said, "Of all the amazing deeds of bravery of the war, I regard MacArthur's personal landing at Atsugi as the greatest of the lot."

That night, at the New Grand Hotel in bomb-blasted Yokohama, Doug started to eat a steak served him for dinner when General Whitney hissed in his ear, "Please don't eat it, General—it might be poisoned!" MacArthur smilingly reassured him, "Don't worry, Court, in Japan the art of political assassination calls for a knife or a gun."

On the bright Sunday morning of September 2nd the battleship *Missouri,* anchored in Tokyo Bay, flew the same American flag that had fluttered over the Capitol in Washington on the morning of the Pearl Harbor attack. Lined aboard in three ranks to witness the surrender ceremony were all commanders of the American armed forces and their allies. There were two honored guests, who had been flown swiftly to Atsugi from their Mukden prison compound, on orders of MacArthur. One was British General Arthur Percival, who had been cruelly mistreated by Yamashita after his surrender of Singapore.

The other man was General Jonathan "Skinny" Wainwright, pathetically thin and weak after years of starvation rations. Shocked and deeply moved at the sight of him, Doug could only embrace him wordlessly. Wainwright quavered, "I—I didn't think the Army would want me back, because I surrendered Corregidor." This was too much for MacArthur. Eyes brimming with tears, he said in a choked voice, "Skinny, as long as I have five stars on my shoulder, you can have command of a corps whenever you want it!"

The dramatic surrender ceremony aboard the *Missouri* was Doug MacArthur's shining hour, and he made the most of it. He compelled the eleven Japanese members of the surrender party to wait on deck for him to appear. Then he faced them in an open-necked shirt, his face stern under his gold-braided cap. As he spoke into a microphone, his tall, erect figure commanded every eye as he towered majestically over the glum Japanese.

"My fellow Americans," he said, "today the guns are silent. A great tragedy has ended. A great victory has been won. The skies no longer rain death—the seas bear only commerce—men everywhere walk upright in the sunlight. The entire world lies quietly at Peace. The Holy Mission has been completed. And in reporting this to you, the people, I speak for the thousands of silent lips, forever stilled among the jungles and the beaches and in the deep waters of the Pacific which marked the way."

MacArthur's deeply troubled feelings about the awesome mushroom clouds over Hiroshima and Nagasaki were reflected in his ringing demand that new ways other than war must be found to settle the disputes between nations. He warned grimly, 'We have had our last chance!"

Finishing his eloquent and moving speech, he told the Japanese to sign the surrender documents on a table in front of them. Prince Shigemitsu, signing for the Emperor and the Japanese government, had difficulty fitting his wooden leg properly under the table. Then he fumbled with his silk hat and white gloves interminably, until he finally put them down. After some apparent trouble with his pen, he looked blankly up and down the paper as though perplexed as to where to sign. His reluctance to acknowledge the first Japanese defeat in two thousand years was obvious to all aboard the *Missouri*.

"Sutherland!" MacArthur loomed wrathfully above the miserable Tokyo prince like Jupiter prepared to hurl a thunderbolt. *"Show him where to sign!"*

When the Japanese had finished putting their signatures on the document, MacArthur signed for the Allies, using a number of pens to complete his name. The first pen went to Skinny Wainwright; the last was a small, cheap red pen which was later returned to its owner, Mrs. Jean MacArthur, who was listening to her husband on the radio in Manila.

The surrender proceedings ended in eighteen minutes, precisely the time Doug had allotted for them. Suddenly a thousand B-29 Superfortresses and a thousand Navy fighters and dive-bombers roared through the skies overhead toward the sacred mountain of Fujiyama—an impressive display of strength that punctuated the end of an unforgettable chapter in American history.

14

MacArthur's Japan

On the day that MacArthur led his occupation forces into Tokyo, a wave of suicide swept through the city. Most Japanese were convinced that the victorious Americans would be as brutal and ruthless as their own troops had been as conquerors. They felt disgraced by defeat, abandoned by the god they had believed in, stripped of purpose in a country that had become a smoking ruin of hunger and unemployment.

"Never in history," MacArthur said later, "has a nation and its people been more completely crushed than were the Japanese at the end of the struggle. . . . Their entire faith in the Japanese way of life, cherished as invincible for many centuries, perished in the agony of their total defeat."

On September 8th the Stars and Stripes were raised again over the American Embassy in Tokyo, which became Doug's home and personal headquarters for the next six years. When Jean and little Arthur, now seven, arrived from Manila, he showed them a portrait that had hung on the walls through the war.

"Know who that is, son?"

"Sure, Daddy. George Washington. He was the father of his country." He thought a moment. *My* country." Jean smiled and hugged him. "Now Daddy is the father of a country, too. *This* country. Just like Washington, he fought and drove out the tyrants, and now he has to rule the country and make sure that it stays free."

Doug suddenly looked tired. "I'm worried, Jean," he admitted. "I've got to make Japan over from top to bottom. These people are still living in the age of feudalism. If I can't lead them into twentieth century democracy—and fast—Russia will certainly give them another choice!"

He set up SCAP Headquarters on the sixth floor of the Dai Ichi "Number One" Building in central Tokyo, overlooking the Palace grounds. On his second day at this office a Japanese carpenter blundered into his private elevator with him, and would have fled in awe if Doug had not insisted on sharing the ride. The amazed carpenter, reflecting on this lesson in democracy, wrote MacArthur a grateful letter, admitting, "I realize that no Japanese general would have done as you did."

The occupation troops in Japan were almost all American, but they officially represented thirteen different Allied nations, including the Soviet Union. Doug had several clashes with the Russians, who tried to give him orders through the Allied Council for Japan. He made it sternly clear that he was open to "suggestions," but only the Supreme Commander himself would decide what orders were necessary and when. He had a clear-cut plan for democratizing Japan, and was determined not to allow Council red tape to slow him down or thwart him.

"Democracy?" the Russians grumbled. "It's dictatorship!"

MacArthur worked in an office without a telephone, facing a picture of Lincoln, his second "personal adviser" inherited from his father. Driving himself relentlessly, he worked seven days a week, even through Easter and Christmas, seldom leaving the office before 8:00 p.m., often staying as late as 10:30.

His hours were extremely hard on his staff, who soon gave up trying to make or keep social engagements. A visiting general from Washington, finding SCAP open and going full blast until late on the Fourth of July, protested to MacArthur that he was "killing" the men by requiring them to work as long as he did. The sixty-five-year-old Supreme Commander snapped impatiently, "What better fate can a man have than to die in the performance of his duty?"

When he did get home for the evening, he would be greeted at the door by Arthur. Throwing his son a five-star salute, Doug would ask, "What is the report today, Sergeant?" Arthur would reply crisply, "All's well, sir!" Then they would go in to the relaxed dinner Jean had ready, after which the three MacArthurs would enjoy a Western film together. When the movie was over and Arthur was tucked into bed, Doug and Jean would usually spend an hour or two alone, during which he often confided the problems that were troubling him.

Unwilling to be distracted from the enormous job of reshaping a nation, MacArthur paid no calls, went to no dinners or social functions, entertained no important visitors except at lunch. In addition to conserving his time and energy, this made him an aloof, secluded, unapproachable figure. MacArthur knew that the Japanese would respect him more if he were seldom seen, just as they stood in awe of the Emperor, who was rarely seen outside of the Palace grounds.

This lonely life was not easy for a lively, sociable young matron like Jean, but she never complained. Devoted to her husband and son, she found her happiness in looking after them. Those Japanese and American wives who knew her found Jean MacArthur a charming, unassuming little woman who never "pulled rank," but always quietly awaited her turn at Army stores and Tokyo shopping centers. The only time the voice of Doug's five-foot, hundred-pound wife rang imperiously was when she tore him away from his luncheon guests with the firm reminder, "Time for your nap, General!"

The Supreme Commander meekly obeyed.

One of MacArthur's first official acts was to import American flour and food for distribution to hungry Japanese, teaching them that a victorious democracy did not believe in a vengeful reign of terror, but in mercy for the vanquished. His next lesson for them was that their Emperor, like all other Japanese, was wholly subject to American authority, for all that he was being permitted to remain on his throne.

To drive this lesson home, Doug commanded the Emperor to appear before him at the Embassy, with no retinue to lend him dignity except an interpreter. Hirohito, "Emperor without peer on the land, the sea, and in the air," was so frightened that he came into MacArthur's presence pale and shaking. The splendidly uniformed ruler lost face further by being received by Doug in an open-necked shirt with no mark of rank. The monarch was told bluntly that he was going to be stripped of his real powers.

MacArthur knew that he would be heavily criticized for allowing Hirohito to remain as Emperor, instead of trying him as a war criminal as the Allied Council wanted. "I can't say this out loud," he sighed to Jean, "but we need him as a figurehead. He's still the spiritual leader of Shintoism. By using him on our side, we can get by with an occupation army of only two hundred thousand men. Without him we'd need two million!"

MacArthur ordered all Japanese troops brought back from the countries and islands they had conquered, and within a year six million were disarmed and demobilized. Imperial General Headquarters, which had waged the war, was abolished, along with all the peerage except for the Royal Family. Doug also outlawed the infamous Black Dragon Society, a terrorist organization that had promoted militarism and the police state.

To teach the meaning of political freedom, he issued a "Bill of Rights" directive establishing free speech, and liberating five thousand Japanese prisoners who were in jail for having expressed "dangerous thoughts." The notorious *Keibei Tat,* a secret force of "thought control" police, was abolished. And, as his father had done in the Philippines almost half a century before, MacArthur introduced the writ of habeas corpus, which did away with secret arrests and illegal imprisonment.

"The police have now ceased to be masters," he reassured the Japanese, "and have become instead the servants of the people."

The Allied Council kept insisting that Hirohito should be named a war criminal and brought to trial. "Why martyr him?" Doug pointed out. "The militarist clique would like nothing better as an excuse to help them raise an underground army. I've got a better idea. You know that Hirohito was so controlled by the militarists that he practically had to get permission to go to the bathroom. They used him to lead the Japanese to war. *We* can use him as a figurehead monarch to lead them to democracy! And to make sure that he stays harmless, well make him admit publicly that he's a man, not a god."

The Council finally accepted MacArthur's logic. He let the Emperor stew in a fever of apprehension and uncertainty as he began a series of arrests of cabinet ministers, generals, and members of the royal household, charging them with war crimes. Among those tried and hung were General Yamashita, commander in the Philippines, and General Homma, who had ordered the Bataan death march. One general taken into custody for atrocities was found to have in his home over a hundred prized military books which he had looted from MacArthur's library in Manila.

The war criminal trials drove home to the Japanese people that Western justice did not hesitate to punish even the highest dignitaries for crimes against humanity. Doug was completely unmoved by influential hints that this or that Japanese ought to be spared. One wife of an American diplomat sighed, "Of course, the trouble with Japan is that all the really *nice* people have been purged." When this remark was reported to MacArthur, he said grimly, "Nice people don't commit atrocities!"

On January 1st, 1946, a glum Hirohito read a New Year's message to the Japanese Diet, and his words were broadcast to the nation. He admitted that he was not divine, and never had been, despite Shintoist teaching that all Japanese Emperors were gods descended from gods. "The ties between us and our people do not depend upon mere legends and myths," he pleaded unhappily. "They are not predicated on the false concept that the Emperor is divine and that the Japanese people are superior to other races and fated to rule the world." The voice was Hirohito's, but the words were Douglas MacArthur's.

The Emperor's swift descent from heaven to earth was no great shock to most Japanese, who had already figured out for themselves that gods don't lose wars or take orders from American generals. But it punctuated MacArthur's order two weeks earlier abolishing Shintoism as a state religion. No longer could the Japanese be made to believe that the individual's life did not count, and that his greatest glory was to die for the Emperor.

MacArthur's next order barred press censorship. One horrified publisher protested that if he dared allow free criticism of the Emperor system in his paper, this crack in the dam might lead to a flood that would sweep Hirohito off the throne. "Any system which can't stand the test of free discussion," Doug replied calmly, "isn't worth keeping."

To prepare the youth of Japan for their new future, he revolutionized the school system. Old school boards were tossed out, along with teachers who could not adjust to the fresh winds blowing from Tokyo. Also dumped were primary grade texts which posed such problems as: "If one machine gun will kill ten Americans, how many will kill one hundred?" New texts were written by Japanese scholars to tell the truth about Nipponese history and the rest of the world.

A new Japanese Constitution, inspired by MacArthur, served to line up the former feudal state with the democracies of the West. The Diet became a British-style Parliament, with full powers, and Hirohito became a powerless constitutional monarch. The bill of rights was made law of the land. The Japanese became the only nation in the world to forbid itself "forever" to make war, and to ban all military forces.

MacArthur brought government closer to the people by changing the laws so that, for the first time, local communities elected their own officials, collected their own taxes, controlled their own police, chose their own school boards. He also introduced the civil service system, and the government jobs were awarded on the basis of merit. Slowly but surely the Japanese began to understand the working of democracy.

One of the biggest bombshells Doug tossed into the old order was his insistence that the forty million women of Japan, who for centuries were nothing more than domestic slaves, should be given the right to vote. At one shrewd stroke he won the enthusiastic support of almost half of Japan's voting population. Following the nation's first free election, thirty-nine women took seats in the new Diet, each happily waving a message of congratulations from Douglas MacArthur.

The Russians in Japan sneered that, whatever other reforms MacArthur might introduce, he would never touch the all-powerful Zaibatsu families—fourteen family clans united in a monopoly that owned 90 percent of Japan's industries. The Zaibatsu had worked hand in glove with the militarists, tolerated no labor unions, enforced slave conditions for their workers, paid not a penny in taxes. How could anyone expect such a striking example of capitalism to be criticized by Americans?

The cynical Russians were amazed and baffled when Doug ordered the Zaibatsu holdings dissolved, and their stocks turned over for re-sale to the public and to workers in the Zaibatsu industries. No Zaibatsu was allowed to buy back a share. At one stroke the Zaibatsu trust was crushed, and Japan had a competitive economy. Not only that but MacArthur levied a 100 percent war profits tax on the Zaibatsu *and* the Emperor.

"Gracious!" Jean laughed when Doug told her. "Back home they'll probably start calling you a Socialist!"

He smiled. "They called Roosevelt one, too. No, I'm still a Republican, but a liberal one in some respects, I hope. When the occupation is over, I think Japan has to be a little left of center. And I hope it will!"

Doug was shocked to learn that in some textile factories near Tokyo, female workers were actually being sold as slaves to factory managers. He promptly saw to it that the Diet passed a law abolishing forced labor, and then "instructed" the prime minister to encourage unionization. One year later no less than four million workers were organized into seventeen thousand unions bargaining collectively with employers, under new labor laws described as "twenty years ahead of those in the US."

MacArthur also introduced Social Security for workers, and announced that his goal was to ensure "the well-being of the entire nation from the cradle to the grave." Nor did he overlook the plight of the Japanese peasants, who toiled as tenants and sharecroppers on the large estates of absentee landlords who gave them only enough to eke out a miserable existence. In a land reform program which Doug called "the most successful experiment of its kind in history," he forced the government to buy the land from its owners, and break it up for resale at low prices to the peasants who worked it.

When 90 percent of Japan's farms had been changed into small individual holdings, MacArthur announced, "The hated system of land tenure, so contributory to general unrest in Asia, has been abolished. Every farmer is now accorded the right and dignity of ownership of the land he long has tilled . . . an invincible barrier against the advance of socialistic ideas." He pointed out privately to Jean that if Chiang Kai-shek had done the same thing in China, land reform would have made it impossible for Mao Tse-tung to have won support for a Red China.

As MacArthur's democratic revolution took hold in Japan, the astonished Japanese found that instead of being punished for Pearl Harbor, their conqueror had led them out of peonage into a bright, happy new world. Worshipping him as their hero and leader, they crowded outside the Dai Ichi Building to catch a glimpse of him, wrote him more fan mail than any Hollywood actor ever received, and even began to venerate him as a god in place of the discredited Emperor. Some Japanese were convinced that Doug himself was partly Japanese, and invented a wild tale that his great-grandmother was born in Kyoto. Others confidently expected that when Arthur grew up, he would be married by his father to a Japanese princess.

Although his popularity in Japan was widespread, MacArthur was too dictatorial for some Japanese tastes. Kazuo Sakamaki, lone survivor of the midget Jap subs that participated in the Pearl Harbor attack, said wryly, "General MacArthur was supreme both in name and fact. Everything he said was taken with resignation. 'We cannot help it.' Pretty soon 'MacArthur' became a common noun. If a housewife dominated and ruled over her husband, the people said, 'Too bad, she is a macarthur!'"

Doug's one-man rule of Japan also did not sit too well with members of the Allied Council. The British representative protested that he treated the Council with "frivolous derision" and another diplomat complained, "MacArthur cannot stand to take advice. It is his greatest defect that he has to do everything alone." The heaviest blasts of criticism came from the Russian representative, Lieutenant General Kuzma N. Derevyanko, who lost no opportunity to needle the Supreme Commander, despite a secret mutual respect and liking between the two men.

In America, meanwhile, a "MacArthur for President" boom was once more underway, with a million voters signing a petition asking that he be made the Republican candidate for the elections of 1948. But Doug refused to come home to campaign, and the boom subsided. He sent word to the Republican Convention in Philadelphia that his name not be considered.

By 1950, when Doug reached his seventieth birthday, a new Japan stood in place of the old. "My administration in Japan is the greatest reformation of a people ever attempted," he declared with pardonable pride, "and the greatest spiritual revolution the world has ever known. . . . As Japan goes, so in due time may go all of Asia. For men will come to see in Japan's bill of rights and resulting social progress the antidote to many of Asia's basic ills."

When the peace treaty with Japan was signed, Prime Minister Shigeru Yoshida sent MacArthur a loser's tribute: "My heart and the hearts of all Japanese turn to you in boundless gratitude, for it is your firm and kindly hand that led us, a prostrate nation, on the road to recovery and reconstruction."

Up until June, 1950, Doug had left Tokyo only twice in five years. The first time he had gone to Manila as guest of honor at the ceremony to mark Philippine independence, at which he said, "Today we have buried imperialism in the Orient."

His second trip, two years later in 1948, was made with Jean to Seoul to mark the birth of another new nation—the Republic of South Korea. For three years after the war this area had been occupied by American troops, while above the 38th Parallel the Russians had occupied North Korea. Now both sides were pulling out of the split country, each leaving behind a satellite government hostile to the other.

MacArthur promised aging, crusty President Syngman Rhee, "I will defend the Republic of Korea, if necessary, as I would my own country, just as I would California." Fortified by this promise, Rhee loudly threatened the Communist puppet regime in North Korea. The North Koreans, meanwhile, quietly built up a powerful army trained and equipped by the Russians. Across the Pacific the United Nations watched these developments uneasily.

In early 1950 Doug was thinking of going home at long last. For one thing, he felt he owed it to Arthur, who was now twelve and had never been to a school with other boys, having been educated by tutors in Australia, the Philippines, and Japan. It also bothered the intensely patriotic MacArthur that his son had never seen their native land.

Doug felt that his job in Japan was largely done, and that there was a vastly bigger task awaiting him at home. As America's greatest war hero, revered by his countrymen, he knew that his advice could influence the nation's thinking about war and peace. He wanted his fellow Americans to understand that now atomic weapons had made war obsolete—that the very survival of mankind depended upon *preventing* any more world wars.

"Could I have but a line a century hence crediting a contribution to the advance of peace," he wrote wearily, "I would gladly yield every honor which has been accorded by war."

But even at the age of seventy MacArthur was not to be allowed to retire from the battlefield. On June 25th, 1950, nine North Korean divisions suddenly thundered across the 38th Parallel in a Communist invasion of South Korea.

"I guess," Jean MacArthur told her son with a sigh, "that we won't be going home for a while yet!"

15

Korea: General of the World's Army

The news reached MacArthur at four o'clock on a Sunday morning. Alerting the entire Far Eastern Command, he ordered all available military equipment rushed to the South Koreans, and took immediate steps to evacuate two thousand American and U.N. personnel stationed in Seoul, the South Korean capital just south of the 38th Parallel.

As a summer storm lashed Tokyo's Haneda airport on June 29th, MacArthur prepared to board the *Bataan* for a flight to the Korean front to study the military situation for himself. A command car came hurtling across the soaked airfield, screeching to a stop at the boarding ramp. Lieutenant General George E. Stratemeyer, chief of the Far East Air Force, jumped out and cupped his hands to his mouth to be heard above the roar of the *Bataan's* motors.

"You can't go, General!" he yelled at the tall figure about to enter the plane. "You don't have any place to land! Kimpo Airport has been captured and the field at Suwan is unsafe!"

MacArthur ordered pilot Major Tony Storey, to cut the engines. "If I don't go, you'd go yourself, George, wouldn't you?"

"Yes, but I don't count. You're a different matter!"

Doug grinned. "We go!" And he waved farewell.

On the flight to Korea he enjoyed the luxury of smoking his old corncob pipe, something he hadn't dared to do in Tokyo because it would cause him to lose face as a "peasant type." Near Seoul a Russian Yak fighter came hurtling through the bleak skies, but was swiftly driven off by four American Mustangs which rose to escort MacArthur. Storey brought the *Bataan* down on bomb-pocked Suwan airfield in a risky but skillful landing.

MacArthur lost no time in touring the front by jeep, a difficult task because the roads south from Seoul were choked with refugees from the burning city. There was a mad surge for the ditches at the side of the road when Red planes swooped down to strafe at treetop level. Standing erect on the road, MacArthur watched thoughtfully through binoculars as a hundred Russian tanks spearheaded the southward drive of six North Korean divisions, unchecked anywhere. Half of the confused South Korean Army was already captured or on the casualty list.

When he had seen enough, he flew back to Tokyo and sent a message to Washington, warning President Truman that the "retreat" of Rhee's armies was, in fact, a disastrous rout. If South Korea was allowed to fall, there would be a distinct Communist threat to both the Philippines and Japan. Truman was deeply worried, suspecting that the Korean conflict was simply a Russian chess move on the board of international strategy. Did Stalin intend to lure us into Korea, knowing this might in turn bring us into conflict with Mao Tse-tung's vast Chinese armies in a war that could last thirty years, draining away all of America's manpower and resources? Stalin thus could, in one deft stroke, bleed to death the two nations he feared most—China and the United States—and leave him free to carve up Europe as he saw fit.

Nevertheless, Truman realized that at least the first steps of such a gamble had to be taken. Stalin could not be allowed to Asiatic mainland, from which he could spring from Korea back into Red China.

On July 31st MacArthur suddenly flew to Formosa and spent a day and a half consulting with Chiang in a visit publicized around the world. Doug had no authority from Washington to do this, but the gesture was widely interpreted to mean that military cooperation between the United States and Chiang was imminent. Truman was shocked and outraged. How *dare* MacArthur take it upon himself to make his own American foreign policy? Didn't he realize that his rash act had embarrassed the US in the United Nations, and given the Red Chinese a pretext for intervening on the side of North Korea?

Doug received word from the White House to do or say nothing further on the question of Formosa. But Truman found, as Roosevelt had before him, that MacArthur was impossible to silence when he believed that he was right. Doug prepared a speech to be read in Chicago at a convention of the Veterans of Foreign Wars in which he challenged Truman's belief that support for Chiang would alienate the rest of Asia.

"Those who speak thus do not understand the Orient," he insisted. "They do not grasp that it is the pattern of Oriental psychology to respect and follow aggressive, resolute, and dynamic leadership." Truman was understandably furious, branding the speech as "dangerous sabre-rattling in a delicate international situation." He ordered MacArthur to withdraw this statement, but a news weekly had already gone to press with the full text. The split between Truman and MacArthur was now embarrassingly public.

With Pusan under siege, and the whole UN campaign in Korea in imminent danger of collapse, MacArthur was convinced that only a daring idea could save his forces. He called his staff together and told them he intended to use his old trick that had dismayed and defeated the Japanese—"hitting 'em where they ain't." The North Koreans would never expect him to attack all the way in their rear, almost as far north as the 38th Parallel. He intended to make an amphibious invasion of Inchon, on the west coast of Korea, thirty miles north of Seoul.

Every officer on the staff was stunned and appalled by the brashness of the plan. The first question thrown at Doug was: "Where are the troops coming from?" He declared he would withdraw the 1st Marine Division from the Pusan beachhead, and strip Japan of its last occupation forces, the 7th Division.

"But, General," a Navy officer protested, "Inchon harbor has thirty-foot tides in the middle of September. Just a few hours after high tide, there's no water as far out as two miles from shore. If we didn't invade or pull out *exactly on time*, our whole fleet would get stuck in the mud flats."

"At least why not postpone the operation until October?" a second Navy officer asked. "The tides are better then."

"Can't," MacArthur said. "I want South Korea back in our hands before the rice harvest. I want the South Koreans to get that crop."

More objections were heard on every side. A Marine officer pointed out that the invasion would have to take place in broad daylight, because of the tides, making the assault forces noticeable and vulnerable. Another staff member warned that casualties might be high because Inchon had a nine-foot sea wall instead of beaches. General J. Lawton Collins, Army Chief of Staff, who had flown in from Washington for the conference, argued that a safer target further south would be Kunsan.

Doug shook his head. "An invasion of Inchon will let us take Seoul in less than two weeks. That will let us pinch off the Reds' supply line to their bases in North Korea. And it will land us back on the 38th Parallel in one hop."

"But the risk of failure, General—"

"—is not nearly as great as if we let our troops continue to bleed to death in Pusan, with no hope of relief in sight. Inchon, gentlemen, will save one hundred thousand lives!"

"But the whole plan is an impossible idea, General!" a Marine officer pleaded. "All of us here think so."

"Obviously," MacArthur said dryly. "It reminds me of when a British fleet under General Wolfe was sent to capture Quebec, and his commanders urged him to leave the St. Lawrence River before they were frozen in for the winter. Instead Wolfe proposed a plan for scaling the cliffs south of Quebec at night. His staff called the idea flatly impossible. Wolfe told them, 'Gentlemen, since youre all sure it cannot be done, the enemy will also think so, and it will not occur to him that we would undertake it. Accordingly, we will scale the cliffs tonight." So the British did, caught the French by surprise, won the Battle of Quebec, and swept the French out of Canada."

There was dead silence in the room when he finished. Doug looked around, smiled, and added calmly, "On September 15th, gentlemen, we will do the impossible."

Just before the invasion, MacArthur sent four cruisers and four destroyers up the west coast of Korea. Entering Inchon harbor, the four destroyers headed for shore to destroy harbor mines and draw the fire of hidden Red shore batteries. The Reds took the bait and opened fire. This pinpointed the batteries for the heavier guns of the cruisers. Then bombers from four American aircraft carriers standing over the horizon suddenly roared into view, blasting every enemy position into stunned silence.

At sunrise Doug watched through field glasses from the bridge of the *U.S.S. Mt. McKinley*. He sucked in his breath sharply as the first wave of the 5th Marine Regiment went into action an hour before high tide, taking a small island two miles offshore, and securing the causeway connecting it with the mainland. Then there was an agonizing twelve-hour wait for the tide to come in again."This is it, Court," MacArthur muttered restlessly to General Whitney as he paced the deck. "Everything depends on what the Reds can rush to Inchon before six tonight!"

When the twenty-nine-foot tide rose again, Marine Colonel Lewis "Chesty" Puller shoved off from the captured island at the head of a swarm of LSTs, and skimmed up to and over the nine-foot sea wall. His men smashed through insignificant but desperate resistance, then plunged ahead toward Seoul. The gamble was won.

Coming ashore right behind the invasion force, a triumphant MacArthur sent word ahead that he wanted to decorate Puller personally. This message reached the tough Marine officer during a bitter battle with Red forces west of Seoul. "We're fighting our way for every foot of ground," Puller panted. "If MacArthur wants to decorate me, he'll have to come up here!" A few hours later a jeep swerved up to the front through bursting mortar shells, and Doug did halt Puller long enough to pin on a medal with a grin and a handshake.

On September 18th the 7th Division landed at Inchon, outflanking the Reds at Seoul from the south and rear. The city was in MacArthur's hands by September 28th. His men retook the entire area the Reds had overrun below the 38th Parallel, capturing 130,000 North Koreans. Like General Wolfe at Quebec, MacArthur had done the impossible, winning enthusiastic plaudits from all capitals of the world except Moscow and Peiping.

President Truman, swallowing his personal pique at Doug, told him, "Few operations in military history can match either the delaying actions where you traded space for time, or the brilliant maneuver which has resulted in the liberation of Seoul." The British Chiefs of Staff sent a message praising the Inchon campaign for "brilliant conception and masterly execution of . . . one of the finest strategic achievements in military history."

MacArthur was forced to halt his troops at the 38th Parallel while the UN debated whether the "police action" was finished, or whether he ought to pursue the fleeing remnants of the enemy into North Korea. On October 7th the UN gave him a go ahead. First, Doug sent word to the Communist leaders of the North Koreans to lay down their arms and cooperate in establishing a unified Korea. When this appeal was ignored, the UN army crossed the 38th Parallel and in a matter of days swept all the way up almost to the Manchurian border.

Only one giant question mark loomed in the path of total victory. On the opposite side of the Yalu River, which marked the boundary between Korea and Red Chinese Manchuria, Mao Tse-tung had massed half a million troops.

On October 15th Doug was summoned to a meeting on Wake Island by President Truman, whom up till now he had never met face-to-face. With the international situation still delicate, Truman wanted to be certain that the impetuous MacArthur would not again do or say anything which would embarrass the administration, as he had in the Formosa affair. When the two men shook hands, outwardly cordial at least, an observer shrewdly characterized the meeting as more like an encounter between two equal heads of state, rather than as a general reporting to his Commander-in-Chief. They talked together privately for about an hour, then met for a longer conference with their staffs.

At one point Truman asked bluntly, "What are the chances of Chinese or Soviet interference?" MacArthur, who had been reassured on this point by information given him by the Departments of Defense and State, as well as the CIA, replied, "Very little. Had they interfered in the first or second month, it would have been decisive. We are no longer fearful of their intervention." In taking leave of Truman at the airport, he said confidently, "The way things are going now, the boys will be home for Christmas."

But soon after MacArthur's forces took Pyongyang, the capital of North Korea, more and more prisoners turned out to be not North Koreans but Chinese "volunteers." It soon became evident that up to sixty thousand of these "volunteers" were crossing the Yalu to help stiffen the battered North Korean army. They led massive counter-attacks, indifferent to the cost in Red lives, and forced the UN troops to begin retreating while Russian-built planes flying from Manchurian bases pounded UN positions.

Furious at Red China's undeclared warfare, MacArthur ordered the bridges over the Yalu destroyed. Before American planes could carry out the order, it was immediately countermanded from Washington by Truman. "I realized for the first time," Doug declared afterwards, "the extraordinary decision which had been made to deny me the use of my full military power to safeguard the lives of my soldiers and ensure the safety of the army. To me it clearly foreshadowed the tragic situation which has since developed, and left me with a shock I had never before experienced."

Trying to keep Red China from entering the Korean conflict in full force, Truman refused to let MacArthur engage in "hot pursuit" of Red planes back to their Manchurian bases, or to bomb Red Chinese supply dumps. The American President also gave Mao Tse-tung his personal guarantee that Manchuria's borders would not be violated by UN troops under any circumstances.

"That does it!" Doug told his aides in disgust. "We've told the Chinese they can't lose, no matter what they do. And at the same time we've made sure *we* can't win!"

Almost a quarter of a million Red Chinese surged into North Korea, advancing like a human tidal wave. They tried to trap four UN divisions, including the famous 7th Marine Division, but MacArthur evacuated his encircled troops by sea. His other forces were swept all the way back south of the 38th Parallel, where they dug in to hold off an enemy who outnumbered them ten to one.

The same voices that only two months earlier had proclaimed Douglas MacArthur the greatest of military heroes for his brilliant Inchon campaign, now cried out that he was a blundering old man who had no more business on the battlefield.

He had "walked into a huge, well-laid trap," had precipitated what might become "the worst military disaster in American history." Correspondents in Tokyo pestered him for an explanation. When he tried to clarify briefly what had happened, a Presidential order was promptly cabled to him from Washington to say nothing publicly that was not cleared first by the Department of Defense.

MacArthur did not long endure this official gag. "We defeated the Northern Korean armies," he later told the American people in a special statement. "Our victory was complete, and our objectives within reach, when Red China intervened with numerically superior ground forces. This created a new war and an entirely new situation. . . . We are required in the midst of deadly war to soften our blows and send men into battle with neither promise nor hope of victory. . . . Why did they start the war if they did not intend to win it? What do they intend to do now—go on piling up our dead indefinitely with no fixed purpose or end in sight? Hardened old soldier though I am, my very soul revolts at such unnecessary slaughter!"

Throughout January, as the war seesawed back and forth in the deadly cold of Korea, MacArthur used his planes, tanks and artillery to inflict heavy losses on the Red Chinese. He kept begging Washington for permission to let him bomb bases in Manchuria, and to use Chiang Kai-shek's Formosan army to invade the Chinese mainland and force a diversion of Red troops and supplies away from Korea. Both requests were denied.

In March MacArthur finally mounted a counter-offensive and drove the Red Chinese back into North Korea. As UN troops, Truman could not ignore the insult to the office of the Presidency implied in MacArthur's appeal to the American people.

But on March 20th he received a message from the Joint Chiefs of Staff telling him to hold the UN army at the 38th Parallel while UN diplomats sought to negotiate a settlement of the conflict with the enemy.

MacArthur was outraged. All the fighting and dying—just to end up back where they had started? In his opinion this proposal was a betrayal of the principles for which thousands of men under him had given their lives. "The Joint Chiefs want to snatch defeat from the jaws of victory," he told his aides ironically. "Mao Tse-tung must be delighted!" He also felt strongly that to allow Communism in North Korea to remain unpunished for its aggression would only encourage further Red adventures in Asia, so that any peace bought by bargaining at the 38th Parallel would not be a real or lasting one.

He openly expressed these views to the press, in defiance of the ban of silence imposed upon him by the President, and repeated them in a letter to Representative Joseph W. Martin, Republican leader of the House of Representatives, adding, "We must win. There is no substitute for victory." Martin threw a bombshell into Congress by reading this letter aloud on the floor of the House on April 5, 1951.

President Truman was understandably furious. He was convinced that the course advocated by MacArthur could only lead the United States into an all-out war with China. He called it "the wrong war at the wrong place at the wrong time and with the wrong enemy," and demanded, "What would suit the ambitions of the Kremlin better than for our military forces to be committed to a full-scale war with Red China?" as well as open disobedience of a Presidential order.

On April 11, 1951 Doug's aide-de-camp, Colonel Sidney Huff, was stunned by a radio flash he heard in his Tokyo apartment. He quickly phoned the American Embassy, and had Jean MacArthur summoned from an official luncheon. In a voice hoarse with emotion he told her what he had just heard.

Truman had issued a public statement: "With deep regret I have concluded that General of the Army Douglas MacArthur is unable to give his whole-hearted support to the policies of the United States Government and of the United Nations. . . . I have, therefore, relieved General MacArthur of his commands and have designated Lieutenant General Matthew B. Ridgway as his successor. . . . General MacArthur's place in history as one of our greatest commanders is fully established. The nation owes him a debt of gratitude for the distinguished and exceptional service which he has rendered his country. . . . I repeat my regret at the necessity for the action I feel compelled to take."

Jean walked quietly back into the dining room. She waited until Doug had finished telling his guests an amusing story, and as the room echoed with their laughter, she bent over him with tears glistening in her eyes and whispered the news in his ear.

MacArthur's face was impassive for a moment. Among the reflections that raced through his mind was the ironic recollection that history was repeating itself for the MacArthurs. Half a century before his father had believed strongly enough in a principle to defy President Taft on a military policy, and had been removed as military governor of the Philippines and sent home. Now Doug MacArthur's career was ending the same way.

He raised his eyes to his wife's tear-stained face, and gave her hand a squeeze. "Well, Jeannie," he said softly through a wry smile, "I guess we're going home at last."

16

Home Comes the Hero

Five years earlier General Kenney had asked Doug when he expected to go home. With only the occupation of Japan on his hands, MacArthur had replied, "When I have finished here, or they fire me. This is my last job for my country." He told Kenney he expected to retire to a house in Milwaukee, where he would rock away contentedly on the porch next to a large pile of stones. Kenney asked what the stones were for. "To throw at anyone," Doug replied dryly, "who comes around talking politics."

But the fact of being dismissed by Truman and abruptly ordered home came as something of a shock, even though he realized that the President could not permit any military commander to defy him publicly. MacArthur may have perhaps expected only the usual fuming rebuke from Washington, not really believing that Truman would dare risk the storm of protest that would surely break over his head if he removed America's greatest military figure from command. But the President had gone even further than that, firing MacArthur publicly in a deliberate attempt to humiliate him. Doug retired to seclusion to think things over while Jean gracefully but firmly fended off the thousands of visitors, phone calls, and cables.

She permitted one message to get through—from ex-President Herbert Hoover, who urged MacArthur to fly home as quickly as possible before his political enemies could discredit him in the eyes of the American people. Doug consented, and when Hoover let this be known in Washington, an official invitation was promptly cabled asking him to address a Joint Session of both houses of Congress on April 19th, 1951. The MacArthurs started packing.

An unexpected visitor showed up on their last day in Tokyo—Emperor Hirohito. Now completely mortal, he wept openly as he bade goodbye to the man who had brought his nation out of the dark ages of feudalism into a prosperous new freedom. The Japanese themselves turned out by the millions, all along the fifteen miles from the American Embassy to Haneda Airport, waving a tearful farewell to the American who had so drastically changed their lives. Clearly moved by this tribute, the still erect, handsome seventy-one-year-old general, said wryly to his wife, "Well, I guess *they* don't think I did too bad a job." Waving to the crowds, Doug, Jean, and Arthur entered the *Bataan,* and Tony Storey whipped the big plane into the skies.

When they touched down at Honolulu, a tremendous crowd had turned out to cheer MacArthur. Jean squeezed his arm and said softly, "See? The *people* don't think you were wrong." Skeptical, he told her with a sigh, "They may be cheering just because they feel sorry for me."

When the *Bataan* flew over the Golden Gate bridge, Doug put his arm around the shoulders of his thirteen-year-old son, who was understandably wide-eyed and excited at his first glimpse of America. "Well, Arthur," he said in a voice taut with emotion, "here we are home at last."

Wildly enthusiastic crowds gave the whole city of San Francisco a Mardi Gras appearance as Americans took to the streets, rooftops, and windows to welcome their hero home. Doug was so stunned by the tumultuous reception that he could hardly stammer more than "God bless America" on the steps of the City Hall.

But even this celebration was dwarfed by the uproar that greeted the MacArthurs in Washington, where half a million people surged to the foot of the Washington Monument to hear and see Doug when a motorcade brought him down Pennsylvania Avenue, escorted by motorcycles and armored cars. "If the American people have anything to say about our history books," a Washington columnist observed, "it's obvious from their reverence for MacArthur that he's going to become one of our folk heroes along with Washington, Lee, and Grant."

When Doug entered the halls of Congress to address the Joint Session called in his honor, the sight of his tall, proud figure in dress uniform brought the whole Congress to its feet in a standing ovation.

Speaking in a strong, clear, ringing voice that conveyed his deepest convictions, Douglas MacArthur delivered what has been called one of the most eloquent speeches ever heard in the halls of Congress.

"I address you," he told his fellow countrymen, "with neither rancor nor bitterness in the fading twilight of life, with but one purpose in mind: to serve my country."

His jaw was grim and his hands trembled when he said, "I have just left your fighting sons in Korea. They have met all tests there, and I can report to you they are splendid in every way. It was my constant effort to preserve them and end this savage conflict honorably and with the least loss of time and a minimum sacrifice of life. Its growing bloodshed has caused me the deepest anguish and anxiety."

He warned Americans against throwing away victory for a false, unreliable peace: "In war there is no substitute for victory. There are some who, for varying reasons, would appease Red China. They are blind to history's clear lesson, for history teaches with unmistakable emphasis that appeasement but begets new and bloodier war. . . . Why, my soldiers asked of me, surrender military advantages to an enemy in the field? I could not answer."

Finally he let the nation see into his heart with this moving farewell: "I am closing my fifty-two years of military service.

When I joined the Army, even before the turn of the century, it was the fulfillment of all my boyish hopes and dreams. The world has turned over many times since I took the oath on the Plain at West Point, and the hopes and dreams have long since vanished. But I still remember the refrain of one of the most popular barrack ballads of that day which proclaimed most proudly that 'Old soldiers never die—they just fade away.' And like the old soldier of that ballad, I now close my military service and just fade away . . . an old soldier who had tried to do his duty as God gave him the light to see that duty. Goodbye."

But the American people had no intention of letting their hero fade away before they could show how they felt about him. When the MacArthurs went to New York City to take up residence in a penthouse suite at the Waldorf Astoria Hotel, a roaring crowd estimated at over seven million welcomed them with a gigantic ticker tape motorcade that made it seem as though the city had been hit by a spring snowstorm. At City Hall the mayor presented Doug with a special gold medal to express "the city's esteem and affection."

So many other cities begged MacArthur to visit them that he decided to make a tour of eleven states in a one-man crusade to arouse Americans to their peril as he saw it. "I have been warned by many that an outspoken course, even if it be solely of truth, will bring down upon my head ruthless retaliation," he declared. "But I shall raise my voice as loud and as often as I believe it to be in the interest of the American people."

Militant extremists of the right wing imagined that he was trying to whip up a war fervor in America. They were soon confused and dismayed, however, to hear him warn, "Modern war is so destructive that it must be outlawed completely. Civilization as we know it will be destroyed if world leaders fail in their responsibility to find a solution to the problems and permit a third world war."

MacArthur's enemies accused him of inconsistency—on the one hand calling for total victory in Korea, on the other demanding that all-out war must not be allowed to develop from the clash between Communism and the West. But in MacArthur's view, a clear-cut victory in Korea could be won with the use of America's air superiority. With that victory would go a Communist respect for American power, which could then be used as a realistic basis for banning war from the world.

Americans knew that Douglas MacArthur was not, and never could be, a sabre-rattling warmonger. They responded to him with a warmth and enthusiasm that moved him greatly. "I shall never forget," recalled Norman Vincent Peale, the noted minister, "the light on General MacArthur's face and the deep feeling in his voice when he said to me, 'They are a wonderful people—the American people—quick, impulsive, generous, wholehearted! You can always trust them and believe in them, for in their hearts they are good and true; in a crisis, they will do the right thing.'"

Even though MacArthur was seventy-two in the presidential year of 1952, Hoover and other close friends begged him to let them nominate him as the Republican candidate at the party's convention in July. Doug refused, but was prevailed upon to deliver the keynote address at the convention, which afterwards selected his former aide as its choice for President—General Dwight D. Eisenhower, who was then elected in November.

Three weeks after the convention Doug MacArthur took off the uniform he had cherished for half a century and accepted his first civilian job as Chairman of the Board of Remington Rand, which later became Sperry Rand. No longer burdened with responsibility for the world's troubles, he relaxed in quiet seclusion with the wife and son he loved.

In 1961, at eighty-one, Doug, who had remained steadfast in his affection for the Filipinos, felt impelled to take a sentimental journey back to the Philippines to say farewell to the people who revered him as a patron saint. Thrilled by his visit, the Manila

Government declared a national holiday in his honor, and the Filipinos staged a celebration lasting a whole week.

MacArthur was touched to the point of tears when he learned that his name was still being carried on the company rolls of the Philippine Army, and that as it was sung out at roll call a master sergeant replied for him, "Present in spirit!" When it was time for him to say goodbye to this people whose destinies had become so strangely entwined with his own, he told them wistfully that he could no longer make them the promise that had become a legend in their history. "The burden of the years," he said quietly, "deems it unlikely that I will, once again, be able to fulfill the vow: I *shall return!*"

The following year the Presidential jet was flown to New York to bring Douglas MacArthur to the White House to visit its new occupant, a young man who had served under him heroically in the Pacific as a PT boat commander. President John F. Kennedy was a Democrat, but he did not hesitate to seek advice from a Republican who he knew understood our problems in Asia better than any living American. Eisenhower, ironically, had not consulted MacArthur because of a coolness between them fanned by Eisenhower's Secretary of State, John Foster Dulles.

Emerging from the White House with a military grace that belied his eighty-two years, Doug replied to newsmen's eager questions by saying simply, "The President and I discussed the world situation and reminisced about our old comradeship in the Pacific war." He recalled Kennedy as a "brave and resourceful young naval officer," and added with a twinkle, "Judging from the luncheon he served me, he seems to be living somewhat higher on the hog these days!" One of the reporters asked whether he felt pessimistic about the world situation. "Completely optimistic," he replied firmly. "Anybody who believes that the United States of America doesn't have a bright future should have his brains examined. We are at the beginning, not at the end!"

Both Houses of Congress unanimously passed a special resolution expressing the "thanks and appreciation of the Congress and the American people" for his outstanding leadership and devotion to his country. House Speaker John McCormack handed him this resolution with praise that recalled all of the great MacArthur battles that were now history—the Marne, Meuse-Argonne, St. Mihiel, Sedan, Bataan, Corregidor, New Guinea, Leyte, Lingayen Gulf, Manila, Borneo, Pusan, Inchon. Hands trembling slightly with age and emotion, Doug expressed his gratitude for this evaluation of his services by Congress "after a lapse of sufficient time to be swayed neither by sentiment nor emotion." But he pointed out that a general was only as good or bad as the troops he led, and declared proudly, "Mine were great!"

The following month President Kennedy asked the Treasury Department to mint a special gold medal in honor of MacArthur. A short while later Doug was called to West Point to accept the Sylvanus Thayer Award given only to those "whose service and accomplishments in the national interest exemplify personal devotion to the ideals expressed in the West Point motto—Duty, Honor, Country." In a stirring address to the long gray line out of which he had risen to greatness, Doug told the future MacArthurs that the true soldier is never a warmonger, but on the contrary "prays for peace, for he must bear the deepest wounds and scars of war." On the eve of his eighty-third birthday MacArthur was asked by President Kennedy to perform still another service for his country. US participation in the 1964 Olympic Games was threatened by a bitter fight between the US Track and Field Federation and the Amateur Athletic Union over eligibility of US athletes. Attorney General Robert Kennedy tried to settle the dispute but failed. A similar squabble had once before almost wrecked US participation, in the 1928 Amsterdam Games, but had been settled by the man who afterwards led the US Olympic team to Holland—Douglas

MacArthur. Now the President asked him to use his prestige as an arbitrator once again. MacArthur agreed, and settled the squabble in quick order.

The magic name of MacArthur seems to gather new luster with each passing year. In March 1963, an angry fight broke out in the Defense Department between the Air Force and the Army over the Army's desire to provide its own air support for ground troops with helicopters. Air Force brass in the Pentagon strove to win the dispute by triumphantly quoting a twelve-year-old statement by Douglas MacArthur: "The support that our tactical air arm has given to our ground troops in Korea has perhaps never been equaled in the history of modern war."

"Hypocrites!" fumed an Army general. "For twenty years the Air Force has tried to drag MacArthur's name in the mud. Now they turn around and try to hitch their wagon to his star. It shows the depths to which the Air Force has sunk!"

"No, it doesn't," his aide replied quietly. "It simply shows how high MacArthur's star has risen."

17

MacArthur—Man and Legend

Few men in their lifetimes have been loved and hated with such intensity as Douglas MacArthur. As a schoolmate at West Point once observed about him, he made either staunch friends or bitter enemies. It was impossible to be neutral about MacArthur. Because his aloof manner made him seem like a lofty warrior on a distant Alp, few drew close enough to know him well as a man. This isolation made it easy for unfavorable legends about him to win credence among civilians as well as men in uniform.

His enemies have described him as swashbuckling, arrogant, egotistical, vain, melodramatic, pompous, pretentious, foppish, grandiloquent. He has been dubbed Julius Caesar of the Pacific, a tin god, an outdated Alexander the Great, a dictator, John Barrymore in khaki, a warmonger, a Mikado, Dugout Doug, and God's Cousin (because of his frequent references to the Deity in his speeches). Many of these unflattering descriptions originated in the Air Force and Navy, where there was fierce resentment to MacArthur's references to "my Air Force" and "my Navy" in war communiques.

Much of the dislike of MacArthur stemmed from his solemn theatricality. He had a flair for showmanship, and a brilliant sense of timing. He understood even better than Churchill, Roosevelt and De Gaulle the inspirational value of striking a dramatic pose on the world stage. A strong individualist like each of them, he relished the highly dramatic situations into which he was thrust by the swift march of events, and played his historical role to the hilt, fully conscious that he was a man for the ages. His speeches may have been florid and rhetorical, but the rhetoric was never empty, the sentiments never insincere. MacArthur said what he believed, and believed what he said. If sophisticates scorned him as "a ham playing to the grandstand," those who revered him found his words a deeply moving source of inspiration.

He had an unquestioned talent for making enemies in high places, and they accused him of running a one-man show, of tolerating none but fawning "yes-men" around him. But MacArthur was far too shrewd to handicap himself with a staff of sycophants who would simply parrot his own views, leaving unchallenged weaknesses of strategy an enemy general could exploit. He always encouraged the same vigorous expression of dissent from his aides that he himself never hesitated to express to his superiors. Once he had carefully considered all arguments, however, he was, indeed, "Sir Boss," and rarely permitted his decision to be questioned or overruled.

Those who knew him most intimately described him as sentimental, emotional, deeply religious, sensitive to criticism, uncomfortable in social groups, essentially shy and retiring. When he liked someone, however, he proved very warm and human with tremendous personal charm. His conversation was so brilliant—and one-sided, as a rule—that visitors frequently left his presence amazed by his intellect. His aides adored him to the point of idolatry; and those handling his press relations zealously censored any news release which did not portray the General as a flawless hero with an untarnished halo.

MacArthur was deeply hurt by many of the unkind things printed about him after World War II, particularly the thrusts which were without any basis in fact. It was some consolation to him to reflect that his two "advisers," Washington and Lincoln, had both their full share of calumny in their day. But MacArthur's wounded sensitivities led him to seclude himself more and more with only those close friends whom he knew he could trust.

Military critics question his infallibility as a great general, pointing out that he failed to anticipate Pearl Harbor; considered Corregidor impregnable; blundered at Buna; and assured Truman that the Chinese would not enter the Korean war. His champions argue that all great military leaders make some mistakes, and these were amazingly few in half a century of successfully outthinking America's enemies. MacArthur's relentless, lifetime study of world history helped him make predictions which were astonishingly accurate, as a rule. When the Allies occupied Germany in 1919, he warned it would create such bitterness that a new armed Germany would arise to seek revenge in a second World War. In 1941, when the Nazi armies were sweeping through the Soviet Union like a great tidal wave, MacArthur alone of the American military firmly predicted that the Russians would be able to beat them back.

Even after the harshest accusations that can be made against Douglas MacArthur are weighed in the balance, they seem petty compared to the titanic role he has played in shaping his country's destiny during the twentieth century. Lieutenant General George E. Stratemeyer, former chief of the Far East Air Force, called him "the greatest leader, the greatest commander, the greatest hero in American history."

A man of strong principles, he was quick to fight for them against the highest authority, regardless of personal disadvantage to himself. In the years before World War II, he fought two presidents and the whole Congress to prevent them from disarming, while Germany and Japan were building war machines. And he was dismissed by a third president, for daring to disagree with Administration policy on Korea. His enemies charged him with egotistical intolerance of any opinion but his own. Closer to the truth, perhaps, was his answer to a newsman who asked what he believed in most.

"The defense of the United States," MacArthur replied simply.

High on the list of his virtues must go his great concern with winning victories at the lowest possible cost in casualties. "To Douglas MacArthur," General Kenney said, "every American life—private to general, soldier or civilian—was something precious to be hoarded at all costs."

General George C. Marshall, who as Truman's Secretary of State was generally considered to belong to the anti-MacArthur camp, nevertheless referred to him as "our most brilliant general." In the opinion of Winston Churchill, distinguished historian as well as great war leader, MacArthur was "a glorious commander." One United Nations diplomat told General Kenney fervently, "Thank God the Soviet Union doesn't have men like MacArthur on *their* side!"

Douglas MacArthur will go down in history as the last of the great war heroes. He will be the last because in a world of push-button warfare, armies are obsolete, and there is no longer any need for colorful battlefield generals. No one understood this truth better than MacArthur himself, and it turned the world's greatest warrior into a crusader for peace.

"I am a one hundred percent disbeliever in war," the frontline hero told his fellow Americans earnestly at the close of his career. "Scientific methods of killing have rendered war a fantastic and impossible method for the solution of international difficulties. . . . We should gear our foreign and domestic policies toward the ultimate goal—the abolition of war from the face of the earth. That is what the great masses of the world long and pray for."

In peacetime as in war, MacArthur continued to evince the same stubborn devotion to principle that once compelled Franklin D. Roosevelt to admit, "Douglas, to me you are a symbol of the conscience of America."

BIBLIOGRAPHY

Greenfield, Kent Roberts, editor. *Command Decisions.* (Department of the Army.) New York: Harcourt, Brace and Company, 1959.

Gunther, John. *The Riddle of MacArthur.* New York: Harper & Brothers, 1951.

Hunt, Frazier. *The Untold Story of Douglas MacArthur.* New York: Devin-Adair Company, 1954.

Johnston, George H. *New Guinea Diary.* Sydney, Australia: Angus and Robertson Ltd., 1943.

Kelley, Frank and Cornelius Ryan. *MacArthur: Man of Action.* New York: Doubleday & Company, Inc., 1950.

Kenney, General George C. *The MacArthur I Know.* New York: Duell, Sloan and Pearce, 1951.

Miller, Francis Trevelyan. *General Douglas MacArthur: Fighter For Freedom.* Publisher not indicated, 1942.

Milner, Samuel. *Victory in Papua.* Washington: Office of the Chief of Military History, Department of the Army, 1957.

Pearl, Jack. *General Douglas MacArthur.* Derby, Conn.: Monarch Books, Inc., 1961.

Pratt, John M., editor. *Revitalizing A Nation.* Chicago: The Heritage Foundation, Inc., 1952.

Schoor, Gene. *General Douglas MacArthur.* New York: Rudolph Field Company Publishers, 1951.

Steinberg, Alfred. *Douglas MacArthur.* New York: G. P. Putnam's Sons, 1961.

Whitney, Major General Courtney. *MacArthur's Rendezvous With History.* New York: Alfred A. Knopf, Inc., 1956.

Index